LORD, TEACH US TO PRAY

LORD, TEACH US TO PRAY
PRAYING FOR RESULTS

Lucille Walker

ISBN: 0-87148-525-7
LOC: 86-062994

©1986, Pathway Press

Pathway Press
Cleveland, Tennessee

INTRODUCTION

You and I have a special invitation to enter into a personal relationship with the great God of the universe. The way we enter into this relationship and the way we maintain it is by the way of prayer. To have our sins forgiven and be born again into the life of the Spirit and be listed in the family of God, we must come to God, confessing our sins and receiving Jesus Christ. This coming, this confessing, this receiving is through prayer.

Thus we begin a great adventure with God in which we grow and develop a life pleasing to Him until He finally takes us to live with Him forever.

Prayer is the way we begin. Prayer is the way we continue. Prayer is the path by which we ultimately triumph.

This book is written to help us to pray.

TABLE OF CONTENTS

CHAPTER I
We Are Commanded to Pray 11

CHAPTER II
Understanding What Prayer Is 19

CHAPTER III
Promises of Prayer 31

CHAPTER IV
Examples of Prayer 43

CHAPTER V
How, When, and Where to Pray 53

CHAPTER VI
Hindrances to Prayer 61

CHAPTER VII
How God Answers 71

CHAPTER VIII
What to Pray For 85

CHAPTER IX
How to Spend a Day in Prayer 95

CHAPTER X
Testimonies of Results of Prayer 111

ACKNOWLEDGEMENTS

The author gratefully acknowledges the following for their permission to reprint copyrighted material.

Marching Orders for the End Battle, by Corrie ten Boom. Copyright, 1969. Used by permission of Christian Literature Crusade.

Destined for the Throne, by Paul E. Billheimer. Copyright, 1983. Used by permission of Bethany House Publishers.

Springs in the Valley, Compiled by Mrs. Charles W. Cowman. Copyright, 1939, 1968. Used by permission of Zondervan Publishing House.

What to Do When You Pray, by Lucille Walker. Copyright, 1983. Used by permission of Pathway Press.

European Action Report, Volume 7, Number 2. Used by permission.

The Hour That Changes the World, by Dick Eastman. Copyright, 1978. Used by permission of Baker Book House.

What Happens When Women Pray, Evelyn Christenson. Copyright, 1980. Used by permission of Victor Books.

Emotions: Can You Trust Them?, by James Dobson. Copyright, 1980. Used by permission of Gospel Light Publications.

Pray, by Ben Haden. Copyright, 1974. Used by permission of Thomas Nelson, Inc. Publishers.

Successful Praying, by F. J. Huegel. Copyright, 1973. Used by permission of Bethany House Publishers.

Quiet Thoughts, by Paul S. McElroy. Copyright, 1964. Used by permission of Peter Pauper Press.

Praying God's Word, by Ed Dufresne. Copyright, 1986. Used by permission of Harrison House.

How to Pray, by R. A. Torrey. Used by permission of Moody Press.

God's Chosen Fast, by Arthur Wallis. Copyright, 1968. Used by permission of Christian Literature Crusade.

The Hidden Life of Prayer, by D. M. M'Intyre. Copyright, 1969. Used by permission of Bethany House Publishers.

Bread Upon Waters, by David L. Lemons. Copyright, 1986. Used by permission of Pathway Press.

How You Can Pray With Power and Get Results, by Lowell Lundstrom. Copyright, 1981. Used by permission of Whitaker House.

Liberating the Leader's Prayer Life, by Terry Muck. Copyright, 1985. Used by permission of Christianity Today, Inc.

Hymns of the Spirit, Edited by Connor B. Hall. Copyright, 1969. Used by permission of Pathway Press.

Baptist Hymnal, Edited by Walter Hines Sims. Copyright, 1940. Renewal, 1968. Used by permission of Broadman Press.

The Amplified Bible, Old Testament. Copyright, 1962, 1964. Used by permission of Zondervan Publishing House.

The Living Bible. Copyright, 1971. Used by permission of Tyndale House Publishers.

The Holy Bible, The New International Version. Copyright, 1973, 1978, 1984. Used by permission of Zondervan Bible Publishers.

In Moments Like These, by David Graham, Copyright, 1980. Used by permission of C.A. Music (Division of Christian Artists Corp.)

CHAPTER I

We Are Commanded to Pray

THE BIBLE IS A PRAYER BOOK

You already own the world's greatest prayer book if you own a copy of the Holy Bible. From beginning to end, from Genesis through Revelation, the practice and power of prayer is recorded.

Just as God's house—the temple, the church—is referred to as a house of prayer, so God's people are called prayer warriors. In Isaiah 56:6 and 7 God promises blessings to all who join themselves to Him, serve Him, love His name, and take hold of His covenant. He says, "I [will] . . . make them joyful in my house of prayer . . . for mine house shall be called an house of prayer for all people."

When Paul wrote the letter to the Ephesian Church to teach them about the Christian warfare and how to be strong and to put on the armor of God so as to defeat our enemy the devil, he emphasized the need for prayer. Read the sixth chapter of Ephesians to learn what the armor of God is like. Then notice what Paul says to do after you get into the armor. He says, "Praying always with all prayer and supplication in the Spirit."

Yes, God's house is a house of prayer for all people, and God's people fight their battles and overcome their enemies with prayer.

We Are Commanded to Pray

One book of the Bible is a special book on prayer. It is the Book of Psalms. These 150 chapters record songs and prayers that the people of Israel sang and prayed. In your devotions pray the psalms. Also in your devotions sing the psalms. Just supply your own tune and sing these prayers and praises to the Lord.

Through your study you will see that the Bible is a book on prayer. It tells us about our need to pray, about people who prayed, and about the great rewards of prayer.

UNDERSTANDING WHAT YOU READ

NOTE: Recall or find these answers from the paragraphs you have just read. You may want to write your answers on a separate piece of paper so as not to mark your book.

In this section we have seen that the Bible is a book about prayer.
1. God said, "My house shall be called a house of _____ for all people."
2. Paul taught the Ephesians that after they had put on God's armor for battle, the way to fight was by _____.
3. The book of the Bible often called the Songbook and Prayer Book of Israel is _____.

Answers on page 135.

GOD WANTS US TO PRAY

We Are Commanded to Pray

Probably the greatest thing that a Christian can do is pray. The most important lesson we can learn is how to pray. Nothing is more essential but often it is most neglected. In both the Old and New Testament we find many invitations and commands to pray. Let us note a few of these:

"Seek the Lord and his strength, seek his face continually" (1 Chronicles 16:11).
"Wait on the Lord" (Psalm 27:14).
"Ask of me" (Psalm 2:8).
"Cry unto the Lord" (Joel 1:14).

"Pray to thy Father which is in secret" (Matthew 6:6).
"After this manner therefore pray ye" (Matthew 6:9).
"Watch and pray" (Matthew 26:41).
"Men ought always to pray" (Luke 18:1).
"Ask . . . in my name" (John 16:23).
"Pray without ceasing" (1 Thessalonians 5:17).
"Pray with the spirit . . . pray with the understanding also" (1 Corinthians 14:15).
"We pray always for you" (2 Thessalonians 1:11).
"Brethren, pray for us" (1 Thessalonians 5:25; 2 Thessalonians 3:1; Colossians 4:3).

If we learn to pray more effectively, we will be able to release God's power for our personal needs and the needs of others. The Apostle James said, "Ye have not, because ye ask not" (James 4:2).

UNDERSTANDING WHAT YOU READ

In this section we have observed that many passages of the Bible call on us to pray.

1. According to the passage cited, how often are we to pray? _____.
2. The one to whom we are to pray is _____ in the name of _____.
3. The New Testament writer who often requested that Christians pray for him was _____.

Answers on page 135.

WHY DOES GOD WANT US TO PRAY?

God wants us to be partners with Him in prayer.

Prayer was a very important part of Jesus' ministry while He was here on earth in His incarnation. Prayer is now the main work of Jesus as He sits at the right hand of God and makes intercession for us (Romans 8:34). The writer of Hebrews says, "He is able also to save them to the uttermost that come unto God by him, seeing he ever liveth to make intercession for them" (Hebrews 7:25).

Prayer is also one of the main ministries of the Holy Spirit—the Advocate, the Comforter, the Paraclete, the Helper. Paul declares, "The Spirit also helpeth our infirmities: for we know not what we should pray for as we ought: but the Spirit itself maketh intercession for us with groanings which cannot be uttered. And he that searcheth the hearts knoweth what is the mind of the Spirit, because he maketh intercession for the saints according to the will of God" (Romans 8:26, 27).

Since prayer is such an important work for Jesus and for the Holy Spirit, God must have many good reasons for wanting us to pray. Let us look at some of those good reasons:

1. **Prayer can be a transforming experience.**

   We kneel as sinners. We pray. We confess our sins; we ask for God's forgiveness; we accept the offer of salvation through the death of Jesus who took our place. We rise forgiven, our names written in the Book of Life. We rise transformed.

   We kneel sick, condemned to pain and possibly premature death because of disease or accident. We plead for healing through Jesus who bore our sicknesses and transgressions and by whose stripes we are healed (Isaiah 53:5). We pray. We rise healed—transformed. A transformed life can be ours through prayer.

   We kneel discouraged. We pray. We rise encouraged.

   We kneel defeated, overcome by our enemies that are far too numerous for us to face. But we pray. We call on the help of the One who said, "Greater is he that is in you, than he that is in the world" (1 John 4:4); and we rise victorious, "more than conquerors through him that loved us" (Romans 8:37).

   We kneel confused, not knowing which way to go. We need guidance from above. We pray and He who promised, "In all thy ways acknowledge him, and he shall direct thy paths" (Proverbs 3:6), speaks to us and says, "This is the way, walk ye in it" (Isaiah 30:21). We rise with direction.

   Yes, a transformed life can be ours through prayer.

2. **Prayer brings growth.**

   Living things are growing things. God wants us to grow.

   Sitting in God's presence causes us to grow to be more

like Jesus. "Beholding [Him we] . . . are changed *into the same* [His] *image*" (2 Corinthians 3:18).

When the disciples saw how important prayer was to Jesus, they requested, "Lord, teach us to pray" (Luke 11:1). In prayer we come to understand God's will. Jesus said that He came not to please Himself but to please the Father and to do His will.

In prayer we grow out of our self-centered ways and into the knowledge of God's way.

3. **Prayer prepares us to reign with God.**

Prayer is the means by which we overcome powers and principalities and the rulers of darkness and spiritual wickedness (Ephesians 6:12). Prayer gives us power to overcome, and Jesus promised, "To him that overcometh will I grant to sit with me in my throne, even as I also overcame, and am set down with my Father in his throne" (Revelation 3:21).

4. **Prayer changes things.**

During most of my life I have been reminded to pray by a little wall plaque that reads: PRAYER CHANGES THINGS. And another that asks: HAVE YOU PRAYED ABOUT IT? You could easily make similar wall hangings as reminders for the members of your household.

Prayer does change things, and often the thing it changes most is us. Consider the experience of Corrie ten Boom as she shares a lesson in forgiveness in a letter to a prisoner who was full of hatred. This is from her book *Marching Orders for the End Battle:*

> During the war in Holland, I helped to save Jewish people, because Hitler wanted to kill them. One day a man came to me, who told me that his wife had also helped the Jews and that now she had been arrested. "She is in the police station and probably she will be put to death. Now there is a policeman who is willing to let her escape, if we pay him six hundred guilders, but I have no money." . . . I collected all the money from my friends and all I had myself, and it was exactly six hundred guilders. I gave it to him to save the life of his wife. But he was a betrayer. . . . five minutes later the enemy came and my whole family was arrested. . . . Hatred came into my heart . . . just as it happened with you. I had given him the last money that I had. But then I read

in the Bible that hatred is really murder in God's sight (Matthew 5:21, 22). . . .

I brought my hatred to Jesus. He forgave me and cleansed my heart with His blood. After the war this betrayer was sentenced to death. I wrote to him: "What you have done through your betrayal caused the death of my eighty-four-year-old father, my brother, his son and my sister in prison. I myself have terribly suffered through your fault, but I have forgiven you everything. This is just a very little example of the forgiveness and love of Jesus. He lives in my heart, that is why I can forgive you. Jesus will also come into your heart and will make you a child of God. Confess your sins to Him. . . ."

Later he wrote me: "I have prayed: 'Jesus, when You can give such a love for the enemy in the heart of someone who follows You, then there is hope for me.' I have indeed confessed my sins to Him. Now I know that I am a child of God, cleansed by the blood of Jesus."

So you see that Jesus used me to save the soul of this same man I had hated so much.

Corrie declares that "When Jesus tells us to love our enemies, He himself gives us the love that He demands from us." And because she was able through prayer to forgive, she was able to help others who needed to forgive and to be forgiven.

UNDERSTANDING WHAT YOU READ

In this section we have considered some reasons why God wants us to pray.

1. In prayer we are partners with _____.

2. The main work of Jesus at the right hand of God is that of _____ or _____.

3. We can say that prayer is transforming because we can kneel as a sinner, and after prayer we can rise as a _____.

4. The person who went to prison for trying to save Jews was _____. She also wrote *The Hiding Place*.

Answers on page 135.

FOR FURTHER STUDY

Ten Boom, Corrie. *Marching Orders for the End Battle.* London: Christian Literature Crusade, 1969.

The Book of Psalms: Holy Bible

SELF-CHECK TEST

Answer the following questions without looking at the test of chapter one. When you finish, grade yourself from the answers on page 138. If you get eight or more answers correct, proceed to the next chapter. If you miss three or more, you should read the chapter again, retake the test, and then go on to chapter two.

Multiple Choice

Circle the letter before the response you believe to be correct.

1. The Bible is a book of . . .
    a. science
    b. folklore
    c. prayer
    d. geography
2. The book of the Bible known as the Songbook and Prayer Book of Israel is . . .
    a. Genesis
    b. Song of Solomon
    c. Revelation
    d. Psalms
3. God said that His house was to be called a house of _____ for all people.
    a. preaching
    b. prayer
    c. singing
    d. fellowship
4. Paul said that Christians are like soldiers, going to battle the forces of Satan, and they need to . . .
    a. know how to argue the Scriptures
    b. know how to take up for themselves
    c. pray all the time
    d. stay clear of the enemy

5. Probably the greatest thing a Christian can do is . . .
   a. develop his mind
   b. develop his talents
   c. develop his prayer life
   d. develop his contacts
6. The main work of Jesus as He sits at the right hand of the Father in heaven is . . .
   a. intercessory prayer
   b. creating
   c. resting
   d. judging
7. We say that prayer is a transforming experience because . . .
   a. we get what we want
   b. we become new; we are changed
   c. it sets a good example
   d. it is universal
8. One of the main benefits of prayer is that . . .
   a. we learn how to get what we want
   b. we come to know what God's will is
   c. we show others that we are Christians
   d. we can memorize different prayers
9. The chapter referred to when the disciples requested of Jesus, "Lord, teach us to pray," was . . .
   a. Luke 11
   b. Matthew 11
   c. John 17
   d. Acts 1
10. Through prayer God gave Corrie ten Boom the power to . . .
    a. escape from prison
    b. help her family escape from prison
    c. keep from going to prison
    d. love and forgive her enemy who caused her and her family to go to prison

CHAPTER II

Understanding What Prayer Is

GOD AND MAN HOLD FELLOWSHIP

The Lord God—Jehovah, the living God—made man. God made man to be able to hear and to speak; God talked with man, and man talked with God.

The first *words* that the Bible records that man heard from the voice of God were blessings and then instruction. In Genesis 1:28, 29, "God blessed them, and God said unto them, Be fruitful, and multiply, and replenish the earth, and subdue it: and have dominion over the fish of the sea, and over the fowl of the air, and over every living thing that moveth upon the earth. And God said, Behold, I have given you every herb bearing seed, which is upon the face of all the earth, and every tree, in the which is the fruit of a tree yielding seed; to you it shall be for meat."

Then God continued His instructions in Genesis 2:15-17: "And the Lord God took the man, and put him into the garden of Eden to dress it and to keep it. And the Lord God commanded the man, saying, Of every tree of the garden thou mayest freely eat: But of the tree of the knowledge of good and evil, thou shalt not eat of it: for in the day that thou eatest thereof thou shalt surely die."

Fellowship Is Broken Between God and Man

We are not told just how long God was able to take pleasure in His creation before sin brought a separation, but we know that in the third chapter of Genesis, man's fall, man's sin of disobedience, is recorded.

After this disobedience, Adam and Eve "heard the voice of the Lord God walking in the garden in the cool of the day: and Adam and his wife hid themselves from the presence of the Lord God amongst the trees of the garden" (Genesis 3:8). The fellowship had been broken. Man hid from God.

Invitation to Restore Fellowship

Read the sad words of God searching for man who was running from his loving Creator: "And the Lord God called unto Adam, and said unto him, Where art thou?" (Genesis 3:9).

Thus begins *the long entreaty for man to return to fellowship with his maker.*

Man was made able to communicate with God. The same God who said "Let there be light," and who said, "Let us make man in our own image," said unto man: *"Call unto me,* and *I will answer thee,* and shew thee great and mighty things, which thou knowest not" (Jeremiah 33:3).

Even though sin had caused a separation between God and man, God extended an ongoing invitation to man—"Incline your ear, and come unto me: hear, and your soul shall live" (Isaiah 55:3). "Seek the Lord while he may be found, *call ye upon him* while he is near: Let the wicked forsake his way, and the unrighteous man his thoughts: and let him return unto the Lord, and he will have mercy upon him; and to our God, for he will abundantly pardon" (Isaiah 55:6, 7).

God invites us to pray. God wants to take "pleasure in his people" (Psalm 149:4). *God waits for us to pray.*

UNDERSTANDING WHAT YOU READ

NOTE: Recall or find these answers from the paragraphs you have just read. You may want to write your answers on a separate piece of paper so as not to mark your book.

In this section you have read that men and women were made to be able to talk with God, hear God, and enjoy fellowship with Him. They were made to be friends with God.

1. Before Adam and Eve sinned they were free to _____ with God.
2. After Adam and Eve sinned they were _____ from God.
3. After they sinned, they were afraid and _____ from God.
4. God's desire was to _____ fellowship with men and women.
5. We come to God through the avenue of _____.

Answers on page 135.

God Makes an Offer to Us

All that belongs to God is offered to us for the asking. "Ask, and it shall be given you; seek, and ye shall find; knock, and it shall be opened unto you" (Matthew 7:7). "Ye have not, because ye ask not" (James 4:2). "Call unto me, and I will answer thee, and shew thee great and mighty things, which thou knowest not" (Jeremiah 33:3).

God commands us to pray. He invites us to share in His boundless, unlimited resources. God puts no limits on our prayers. Why don't we have God's good gifts? We don't pray; we don't ask. Why are we powerless? We don't pray. We turn down God's offer.

God commands, "Ask, and it shall be given you . . . If ye then, being evil, know how to give good gifts unto your children, how much more shall your Father which is in heaven give good things to them that ask him?" (Matthew 7:7, 11).

Why am I not making progress in my Christian life? Neglect of prayer. Why do I have so little fruit in my life? Neglect of prayer. We have not because we ask not.

The apostles said, "We will give ourselves continually to prayer, and to the ministry of the word" (Acts 6:4). The secret is stated again in Acts 2:42, "They continued stedfastly . . . in prayers."

"Call upon me," God invites "I will deliver thee, and thou shalt glorify me" (Psalm 50:15).

"Is any among you afflicted? *let him pray*. . . . Is any sick among you? let him call for the elders of the church; and *let them pray over him,* anointing him with oil in the name of the Lord: And the prayer of faith shall save the sick, and the Lord shall raise him up; and if he have committed sins, they shall be forgiven him. Confess your faults one to another *and pray* one for another, that ye may be healed. The effectual fervent prayer of a righteous man availeth much" (James 5:13-16).

God promises: "If my people, which are called by my name, shall humble themselves, and *pray,* and seek my face, and turn from their wicked ways; then *will I hear* from heaven, and *will forgive* their sin, and *will heal* their land" (2 Chronicles 7:14).

Many other times in God's Holy Word He urges us to pray. Some further examples can be found in Ephesians 6:18; Luke 21:36; 1 Timothy 2:8, Matthew 21:22; 1 Peter 4:7; John 14:13, 14; John 16:24; Jeremiah 29:13, 14; Psalm 34:4.

As you read your Bible look for other invitations to pray.

God asks, "Why will ye die?" (Jeremiah 27:13). "Repent, and turn yourselves" (Ezekiel 14:6). "Seek ye the Lord while he may be found, call ye upon him while he is near: Let the wicked forsake his way, and the unrighteous man his thoughts: and let him return unto the Lord, and he will have mercy upon him; and to our God, for he will abundantly pardon" (Isaiah 55:6, 7).

Look at the many things God is offering to those who come to Him in prayer. He offers open doors, answers, the revelation of great and mighty truths, deliverance from our enemies, healing, salvation, forgiveness, pardon, direction, protection, power, and whatever else we need to cause us to be pleasing to Him.

UNDERSTANDING WHAT YOU READ

In this section we have looked at just a few of the offers God makes to those who obey Him and who pray.

1. God promises that as we seek we shall _____ and if we knock it shall be _____ to us.
2. God promises that if you will call on Him, He _____.
3. When the apostles continued to pray and minister the Word, _____ of believers were added to the Lord.
4. God tells us to confess our faults and pray for one another that we may be _____.

Answers on page 135.

Examples of Prayer

O God, save me!

Now I lay me down to sleep. I pray the Lord my soul to keep.

Thank You for the food we are about to receive.

Lord, have mercy on me.

Jesus, I love You.

Father, forgive me; I'm sorry. I confess my sin. I ask You to forgive me for Jesus' sake.

Our Father which art in heaven,
Hallowed be thy name.
Thy kingdom come.
Thy will be done in earth,
As it is in heaven.
Give us this day our daily bread.
And forgive us our debts,

As we forgive our debtors.
And lead us not into temptation,
But deliver us from evil:
For thine is the kingdom, and the power,
And the glory, for ever. Amen
(Matthew 6:9-13, the Lord's Prayer).

We all recognize these as prayers. Here are some other brief examples of prayers:

Lord, help me to remember that nothing is going to happen today that You and I together can't handle.

Help me to remember that the value of service is not measured by the time, but by the quality of obedience it represents, the standard of love, and the extent of sharing of the life of Christ.

Grant us ears to hear, eyes to see, wills to obey, hearts to love.

Grant, O Lord, that we may live in Your fear, die in Your favor, rest in Your peace, rise in Your power, reign in Your glory.

Bless all who worship thee. With thy love, inspire us; by thy spirit, guide us; by thy power, protect us; in thy mercy receive us now and always.—Ancient Collect

Please give me what I ask, dear Lord,
If You'd be glad about it.
But if You think it's not good for me,
Please help me do without it.

Lord, lay some soul upon my heart, And love that soul through me; And may I bravely do my part to win that soul for Thee
("Lord, Lay Some Soul Upon My Heart,"
Baptist Hymnal *p. 332*).

We could go on and on quoting samples of prayers. Many are found in the songs we sing. The bedtime prayers your parents taught you as a child were your first prayers before you were called on to pray your own original prayers.

Also, you can recall the table prayers, the blessings on the food, and the thanks the family gave before eating.

In some countries prayers before meals are sung. We lived in Germany several years and I enjoyed very much the singing of thanksgiving around the table before and after the meal.

When we visited the churches in England we purchased in an old bookstore a copy of one of the prayer books of the Church of England. For a literary friend of ours it was a treasure. Check your public library for collections of great prayers.

But since prayer is much more than memorized prayers or the reading of famous prayers of others, let us examine further what prayer is.

What Is Prayer?

Prayer is first recognizing that God is. Then it is coming into His presence in repentance, confessing our sins and our need of Him. Prayer is humbling ourselves in worship of the holy God of heaven, our Creator, our Father, and accepting His loving forgiveness.

Prayer is acknowledging God; prayer is talking with God. Prayer is listening to God. Prayer is praising God; prayer is loving God. Prayer includes obeying God. Prayer is waiting on God.

Prayer is crying out for help. Prayer is faith speaking out. Prayer is the Word of God becoming alive in us and flowing out through us.

A survey was made of many faiths, of many religious groups. The one thing that they all practiced was prayer. Every religious group believed in prayer and nearly every religious person practiced prayer regularly, usually daily.

We are saved by prayer—the prayer of repentance, confession, acceptance of Christ's sacrifice for us.

Prayer is the channel through which all good flows from God to man—forgiveness, healing, power, love. Prayer is a way of knowing God.

Prayer is a privilege, a means, a duty, a condition, a channel of touching God. One teacher says prayer is worship, work, and warfare. He says it is in the place of prayer that we engage the devil; but we engage him with the victory already won for us on Calvary. We do warfare with the enemy in the authority of the crucified, risen, and ascended Lord.

Moody said that a lad once gave him a great answer to the question—"What is prayer?" The lad answered, "Prayer is an offering up of our desires unto God for things agreeable to His will, in the name of Christ, with confession of our sins and thankful acknowledgement of His mercies."

Paul Billheimer in his book, *Destined for the Throne,* says, "The prayer closet is the arena which produces the overcomer." He says the church through the weapons of prayer is engaged in on-the-job training for her place in reigning with Christ after Satan's final defeat.

Yes, prayer is warfare against the devil. And prayer is one of the greatest tools of the Christian.

Prayer is like a school also. You begin with A, B, C and you keep learning all of your life. It is simple and yet it is unlimited. A child can pray, and yet the greatest saint never learns all there is to prayer.

Prayer not only changes events and circumstances, but prayer also changes the one who prays. It makes the one who prays to become a partner with God. Yes, prayer is a partnership; it is a partnership of God and man working together.

Prayer is universal. That means that it is found everywhere. It is found wherever man is found and in as many languages as there are in the world. Prayer is man's pull back to God; it is the natural expression of man's need and longing for his Creator.

Prayer is not mere repetition of words or mechanical parroting. It is not just quoting the Lord's Prayer or saying memorized words. Prayer is not simply saying "Thank You for the food we eat" or "Now I lay me down to sleep, I pray the Lord my soul to keep." It is also not trying to bend the will of God to our will.

Prayer is coming into the presence of God in the name of Jesus. It is offering our desires to Him. It is seeking His will instead of our own. Pastor Cho of Korea instructs his people to "pray until you touch God." True prayer is seeking God himself.

UNDERSTANDING WHAT YOU READ

In this section you have found several definitions of prayer. Recall or find the answer in the paragraphs you have just read.

1. The prayer that begins "Our Father which art in heaven, Hallowed be thy name" is called _____ _____.
2. Prayer is coming into the _____ of God.
3. Prayer is the channel through which good flows from _____ to man.
4. One teacher says prayer is _____ work, and warfare.
5. Prayer is also like a _____ where you keep learning all your life.

Answers on page 135.

Further Aspects of Prayer

The center of prayer is God. We should not focus on our problems, our needs, or even the needs of others. We should focus on God. Loving Him, listening to Him, worshiping Him, obeying Him, thanking Him, praising Him should be the heart of prayer. This makes prayer positive and powerful.

God's will is the goal of prayer. Prayer is saying yes to God. It is keeping His face before us. It is letting Him open our lips and inspire our requests. It is letting Him set our desires. It is getting to know God and understanding His will and purpose in our life.

Prayer works because God answers. Prayer works because God is alive and He loves every human being. God is a personal, living, loving Father who wants to do wonderful things through us and for us. That is why prayer is such a great force. God is at the other end of prayer.

Prayer brings the natural, the fleshly, the earthly and submits it to the will of God.

Because man was made both for this world and for another world we maintain communication between the two worlds by means of prayer. Because man has sinned and is a sinner he confesses his sin in prayer and God forgives and gives him a new birth—he is born again spiritually. Through prayer man's relationship is reestablished with the holy God. And because man is part of society he prays for others. We pray for ourselves and we pray for others.

Prayer is thanksgiving, gratitude, praise, and adoration. Prayer is commitment. Prayer is believing God, rejoicing in God. *It is the heart of religion*—of salvation. It is contact with the divine Presence. It is living communion with God. It is surrender—self-surrender—of our life to His Life. It is getting self out of the way so that God's will and purpose and love can flow through us. *It is the journey from self to God.* Through prayer we come into the experience of the living Christ.

Since it is all of this, why do we not pray more?

UNDERSTANDING WHAT YOU READ

In this section we have considered further aspects of prayer. Recall or find these answers in the paragraphs you have just read.

1. The center of prayer is _____.
2. The goal of prayer is _____.
3. When we pray, we should not focus on our problems and our needs, but we should focus on _____.
4. Because man was made both for this world and for another world, we can maintain _____ between the two worlds by means of _____.
5. Prayer is the journey from _____ to God.
6. Prayer works because God is _____ and He _____.

Answers on page 135.

FOR FURTHER STUDY

Huegel, F. J. *Successful Praying.* Grand Rapids: Zondervan Publishing House, 1967.

Billheimer, Paul. *Destined for the Throne.* Harrisonburg, VA: Christian Light Publication, Inc., 1975.

SELF-CHECK TEST

Answer the following questions without looking at the text of chapter two. When you finish, grade yourself from the answers on page 138. If you get eight or more answers correct, proceed to the next chapter. If you miss three or more, you should read the chapter again, retake the test, and then go on to chapter three.

Multiple Choice

Circle the letter before the response you believe to be correct.

1. The first words that man heard God speak were words of . . .
    a. blessing
    b. law
    c. warning
    d. instruction
2. Fellowship between God and man was broken by . . .
    a. misunderstanding
    b. disobedience
    c. forgetfulness
    d. weakness
3. After Adam and Eve sinned, they were afraid and their response to God's presence was to . . .
    a. come to Him as before
    b. pretend they did not hear Him
    c. hide from Him
    d. deny what they had done
4. God made an offer to man to . . .
    a. let him go back to the garden
    b. answer him when he prays
    c. forget he ever sinned
    d. overlook the sin

5. The Bible says that if any are sick let them call for the elders of the church who will anoint them with oil and . . .
   a. take them to the doctor
   b. comfort them
   c. pray over them
   d. take them to the church

6. God promises that if His people will humble themselves and pray, seek His face and turn from wickedness, He will do *three things* for them—He will . . .
   a. smile, look the other way, and forget their wrongs
   b. hear them, forgive them, and heal their land
   c. make a list, test them, and consider their request
   d. send the pastor, the evangelist, and the youth director

7. Think about your first prayers. Can you remember your first prayers? Think about how they helped you. Were they prayers for . . .
   a. bedtime
   b. meals
   c. repentance
   d. call for help

8. A study was made of many religious groups. The one thing they all did was . . .
   a. had Sunday services
   b. read the same Bible
   c. prayed
   d. baptized believers

9. When we say that prayer is universal, we mean that . . .
   a. it is found everywhere
   b. everybody does it
   c. it is the same everywhere
   d. it is to the same person

10. Do you know by memory the Lord's Prayer (Matthew 6:9-13)? The correct answer is (d). Practice until you can circle (d).
    a. not yet
    b. some of it
    c. almost all of it
    d. yes

CHAPTER III

Promises of Prayer

One of the main reasons that prayer is such a powerful force is that it is based on the promises of God. And the promises of God will still endure even if heaven and earth should pass away. Passages of Scripture that tell us this are found in Matthew 5:18 and in Luke 17:17. The exact words of Luke are: "It is easier for heaven and earth to pass, than one tittle of the law to fail." And a tittle is just the smallest part, like a dot or a point, or an accent mark.

Solomon, the wisest of all kings, said, "Blessed be the Lord . . . there hath not failed one word of all his good promise" (1 Kings 8:56).

God Keeps His Promises

Jesus came to us as the fulfillment of many promises made to us by God. Just one of those promises is the beautiful one found in Isaiah 9:6, 7: "For unto us a child is born, unto us a son is given: and the government shall be upon his shoulder: and his name shall be called Wonderful, Counsellor, The mighty God, The everlasting Father, the Prince of Peace. Of the increase of His government and peace there shall be no end."

The Holy Spirit came to us by the promise of God. Jesus said in Luke 24:49, "And, behold, I send the promise of my Father upon you: but tarry ye in the city of Jerusalem, until ye be endued with power from on high." On the Day of Pentecost the Apostle Peter reminded the people that the coming of the Holy Spirit in mighty baptism was the fulfillment of the promise made through the prophet Joel: "And it shall come to pass in the last days, saith God, I will pour out of my Spirit upon all flesh" (Acts 2:17). Peter's sermon in Acts 2:14-21 refers to the writings in Joel 2:28-32 of the Old Testament.

Many of our greatest blessings and expectations have come to us through promises made to us by God. Forgiveness now and eternal life with God in heaven are part of God's good promises.

The children of Israel inherited the "Promised" Land. David became king as God promised. Hannah gave birth to baby Samuel as God promised.

The Lord Jesus Christ is coming back for us according to His promise. In Acts we read: "He shewed himself alive after his passion by many infallible proofs, being seen of them forty days, and speaking of the things pertaining to the kingdom of God . . . . And when he had spoken these things, while they beheld, he was taken up; and a cloud received him out of their sight. And while they looked stedfastly toward heaven as he went up, behold, two men stood by them in white apparel; Which also said, Ye men of Galilee, why stand ye gazing up into heaven? this same Jesus, which is taken up from you into heaven, shall so come in like manner as ye have seen him go into heaven" (Acts 1:3, 9-11).

Heaven is ours by the promise of Jesus: "Let not your heart be troubled: ye believe in God, believe also in me. In my Father's house are many mansions . . . I go to prepare a place for you. And if I go and prepare a place for you, I will come again, and receive you unto myself; that where I am, there ye may be also" (John 14:1-3).

The writer of the Book of Hebrews reminds us: "Let us hold fast the profession of our faith without wavering; for he is faithful that promised" (10:23).

PROMISES OF PRAYER

UNDERSTANDING WHAT YOU READ

NOTE: Recall or find these answers from the paragraphs you have just read. You may want to write your answers on a separate piece of paper so as not to mark your book.

In this section you should have discovered that prayer is powerful because it is based on promises written in the Holy Bible.

Complete the answers in these statements.

1. It is easier for _____ and _____ to pass away, than for one word or one letter of _____ promises to fail.
2. A great wise king named _____ said: "There hath not failed one _____ of all his good _____."
3. The Holy Spirit came to us by the _____ of God.
4. Jesus said, "Behold I send the _____ of my Father upon you" (Luke 24:49).
5. The promise of the Holy Spirit was recorded in the Old Testament in the Book of _____.
6. The land of Israel was called the _____ Land.
7. The writer of the Book of Hebrews said that we should hold fast to our faith and not waiver (not give up) because the one who promised is _____. That means we can trust him; He keeps His promises.

Answers on page 135.

The Testimony of George Muller

George Muller was a great man of faith who lived in England in the 1800s. God gave him the desire to care for orphans and to send out missionaries. He was a man of prayer who trusted God to supply all their needs. In a written testimony he shared how his method of praying and believing

God was built on the Word of God and the promises of God:

It has pleased the Lord to teach me a truth, the benefit of which I have not lost for more than fourteen years. The point is this: I saw more clearly than ever that the first great and primary business to which I ought to attend every day was *to have my soul happy in the Lord.*

The first thing to be concerned about was not how much I might serve the Lord; but how I might get my soul in a happy state, and how my inner man might be nourished. For I might seek to set the truth before the unconverted, I might seek to benefit believers . . . I might in other ways seek to behave myself as it becomes a child of God in this world; and yet, not being happy in the Lord, and not being strengthened in my inner man day by day, all this might not be attended to in the right spirit. Before this time my practice had been, at least for ten years previously, as an habitual thing to *give myself to prayer* after having dressed myself in the morning. Now I saw that the most important thing I had to do was *to give myself to the reading of the Word of God, and to meditate on it,* that thus my heart might be comforted, encouraged, warmed, reproved, instructed; and that thus, by means of the Word of God, whilst meditating on it, my heart might be brought into experimental communion with the Lord.

I began therefore to meditate on the New Testament from the beginning, early in the morning. The first thing I did, after having asked in a few words the Lord's blessings upon His precious Word, was to begin to meditate on the Word of God, searching as it were every verse to get a blessing out of it, not for the sake of the public ministry of the Word, not for the sake of preaching upon what I had meditated upon, but for *obtaining food for my own soul.*

The result I have found to be almost invariably this, that after a few minutes my soul has been led to confession, or to thanksgiving, or to intercession, or to supplication; so that, though I did not as it were give myself to prayer, but to meditation, yet it turned almost immediately more or less into prayer. When thus I have been for a while making confession or intercession or supplication, or have given thanks, I go on to the next words or verse, turning all as I go into prayer for myself or others as the Word may lead to it, but still continually keeping before me that *food for my own soul is the object of my meditation.*

Formerly I often spent a quarter of an hour, or half an hour, or even an hour on my knees, before being conscious of having derived comfort, encouragement, humbling of soul, etc., and often, after having suffered much from wandering of mind for the first ten minutes, or a quarter of an hour, or even half an hour, I only then began really to pray. I scarcely ever suffer now in this way; for my heart being nourished by the truth, being brought into experimental fellowship with God, I speak to my Father and to my Friend (vile though I am and unworthy) about the things that He has brought before me in His precious Word. It often now astonishes me that I did not sooner see this point.

It should be noted that by means of prayer and faith and obedience, George Muller supported more than 2,100 orphans and 200 missionaries. And his life continues to be an inspiration to all who learn of him. He dared to trust the promises of God, and the whole story of his life is a testimony that God keeps His promises.

UNDERSTANDING WHAT YOU READ

In this section you should understand an important lesson that George Muller learned from the Lord.

Complete the statements.

1. George Muller said that the first business of every day was "to have my _____."
2. Before this time, he simply prayed; now he reads his _____ as he prays.
3. Then he _____ on what he read in the Bible. This meant that he spent time thinking about what he read.
4. Meditating on the Bible caused him to _____ as the Bible directed.

Answers on page 135.

Consider Some of God's Prayer Promises

Consider these promises of the Scriptures. They will provide the basis for believing when you pray.

He Promises to Respond

"Ask, and it shall be given you; seek, and ye shall find; knock, and it shall be opened unto you: For every one that asketh receiveth; and he that seeketh findeth; and to him that knocketh it shall be opened" (Matthew 7:7, 8). "Call unto me, and I will answer thee" (Jeremiah 33:3).

He Promises Joy

Jesus said: "Hitherto have ye asked nothing in my name:

ask, and ye shall receive, that your joy may be full" (John 16:24).

He Promises Wisdom

"If any of you lack wisdom, let him ask of God, that giveth to all men liberally, and upbraideth not; and it shall be given him" (James 1:5).

He Promises Mercy and Pardon

"Seek ye the Lord while he may be found, call ye upon him while he is near: Let the wicked forsake his way, and the unrighteous man his thoughts: and let him return unto the Lord, and he will have mercy upon him; and to our God, for he will abundantly pardon" (Isaiah 55:6, 7).

He Promises the Holy Spirit

"If ye then, being evil, know how to give good gifts unto your children: how much more shall your heavenly Father give the Holy Spirit to them that ask him?" (Luke 11:13).

He Promises Children

"For this child I prayed; and the Lord hath given me my petition which I asked of him" (1 Samuel 1:27).

He Promises Protection

"For in the time of trouble he shall hide me in his pavilion" (Psalm 27:5). "As for me, I will call upon God; and the Lord shall save me. Evening, and morning, and at noon, will I pray, and cry aloud: and he shall hear my voice. He hath delivered my soul in peace from the battle that was against me" (Psalm 55:16-18).

He Promises Peace and Blessing

The priestly benediction prayed upon the people of God is concluded with the promise of God to bless his people:

And the Lord spake unto Moses, saying, Speak unto Aaron and unto his sons, saying, On this wise ye shall bless the children of Israel, saying unto them, The Lord bless thee: and keep thee: and be gracious unto thee: The Lord lift up his countenance upon thee, and give thee peace. And they shall put my name upon the children of Israel; and I will bless them (Numbers 6:22-27).

He Promises Victory

"But thanks be to God, which giveth us the victory through our Lord Jesus Christ. Therefore, my beloved brethren, be ye stedfast, unmoveable, always abounding in the work of the Lord, forasmuch as ye know that your labour is not in vain in the Lord" (1 Corinthians 15:57, 58).

He Promises Deliverance From Fear

"I sought the Lord, and he heard me, and delivered me from all my fears" (Psalm 34:4). "In my distress I cried unto the Lord, and he heard me" (Psalm 120:1).

He Has Unlimited Resources

Therefore I say unto you, *What things soever* ye desire, when ye pray, believe that ye receive them, and ye shall have them" (Mark 11:24).

"And this is the confidence that we have in him, that, if we ask *any thing according to his will,* he heareth us: And if we know that he hear us, *whatsoever* we ask, we know that we have the petitions that we desired of him" (1 John 5:14, 15).

"Beloved, if our hearts condemn us not, then have we confidence toward God. And whatsoever we ask, we receive of him, because we keep his commandments, and do those things that are pleasing in his sight" (1 John 3:21, 22).

"Now unto him that is able to do exceeding abundantly above all that we ask" (Ephesians 3:20).

He Promises Eternal Life

"Then Peter said, Lo, we have left all, and followed thee. And he [Jesus] said unto them, Verily I say unto you, There is no man that hath left house, or parents, or brethren, or wife, or children, for the kingdom of God's sake, Who shall not receive manifold more in this present time, and in the world to come life everlasting" (Luke 18:28-30).

"My sheep hear my voice, and I know them, and they follow me: And I give unto them eternal life; and they shall never perish, neither shall any man pluck them out of my hand" (John 10:27, 28).

UNDERSTANDING WHAT YOU READ

In this section you should have been impressed with some of the many benefits God promises you when you pray.

Fill in these blanks for review and emphasis:
1. "Ask, and ye shall receive that your _____ may be full" (John 16:24).
2. "I sought the Lord and he heard me and _____ me from all my fears" (Psalm 34:4).
3. "We know that we have the _____ that we desired of him" (1 John 5:14, 15).
4. "Ask of me and I will give thee the _____ for thine inheritance" (Psalm 2:8).
5. If evil man knows how to give good gifts to his children, how much more will God give _____ to His children who ask (see Luke 11:13).
6. We have confidence that if we ask anything _____ _____, he heareth us (1 John 5:14).

Answers on page 135.

The Testimony of the Apostle Paul

Paul was arrested in Jerusalem and the Sanhedrin desired to have him killed. More than 40 men went to the priests and told them they had taken a solemn oath not to eat anything until they had killed Paul. They set up a plot to ambush him on his transfer from Jerusalem to Caesarea.

But the Lord stood near Paul and said, "Take courage! As you have testified about me in Jerusalem, so you must also testify in Rome." The Lord made an appointment for Paul at the emperor's palace in Rome.

Satan tried to stop God's plan but God is able to bring good even out of Satan's devices.

The high priest and the elders went to Caesarea to accuse Paul. God turned the trials into testimonies before the highest rulers of the land with their wives and their courts. King Agrippa's own words were, "Almost thou persuadest me to be a Christian" (Acts 26:28).

Satan did not give up. On the way to Rome with other prisoners, 276 people on board, a wind of hurricane force swept down upon them.

The storm was so terrible that they finally gave up hope of being saved (Acts 27:20).

But an angel of the Lord stood by Paul in the night and said, "Fear not, Paul; *thou must be brought before Caesar:* and, lo, God hath given thee all them that sail with thee. Wherefore, sirs, be of good cheer: for I believe God, that it shall be even as it was told me" (Acts 27:24, 25).

More stormy days followed, shipwreck resulted, but everyone escaped safe to land.

After all that, one would think that Satan would give up and let Paul get to Rome. But there was soon to be another attempt to end Paul's life. Again Satan used a serpent. Out of the sticks that Paul gathered to add to the fire to warm them from the rain and cold, a viper fastened itself on his hand.

The islanders watched Paul and waited for him to fall dead from the poisonous bite. They whispered among themselves, "This man must be a murderer, for even though he escaped the sea, justice won't permit him to live." God, however, protected Paul. Paul just shook the snake off and suffered no harm. After watching a long time and seeing that the snake had no harmful effect on Paul, they decided he must be a god. After Paul prayed for the father of Publius the chief official of the island, and he was healed, the islanders brought the rest of the sick to Paul, and they were healed (Acts 28:3-9).

So great was the testimony of Paul's relationship to God that when he did arrive in Rome, he was allowed to rent his own house with a soldier that kept him.

The Book of Acts ends by recording, "And Paul dwelt two

whole years in his own hired house, and received all that came in unto him, Preaching the kingdom of God, and teaching those things which concern the Lord Jesus Christ, with all confidence, no man forbidding him" (28:30, 31).

God keeps His promises!

FOR FURTHER STUDY

The Book of Acts: Holy Bible

Cowman, Mrs. Charles. *Springs in the Valley.* Grand Rapids: Zondervan, 1968.

SELF-CHECK TEST

Answer the following questions without looking at the text in chapter three. When you finish, grade yourself from the answers on page 138. If you get eight or more answers correct, proceed to the next chapter. If you miss three or more, you should read the chapter again, retake the test, and then go on to chapter four.

Multiple Choice

Circle the letter before the response you believe to be correct.

1. Prayer is a powerful force because it is based on the promises of . . .
   a. great philosphers
   b. wealthy investors
   c. military leaders
   d. faithful God

2. The book in the Bible that reminds us that "he is faithful that promised" is . . .
   a. Acts
   b. Hebrews
   c. John
   d. Genesis

3. The Old Testament book that promised the outpouring of the Holy Spirit is . . .
   a. Ezekiel
   b. Joel
   c. Amos
   d. Deuteronomy

4. The Promised Land of the Old Testament was the land of . . .
   a. Egypt
   b. Lebanon
   c. Israel
   d. Jordan
5. The main theme of this chapter is . . .
   a. God keeps His promises
   b. Jesus is coming again
   c. we will live with Jesus in heaven
   d. testimonies of people who believed God's promises
6. George Muller found that what helped him most in his prayer life was . . .
   a. spending time
   b. reading and meditating on the Word
   c. confessing his needs
   d. interceding for others
7. One of the key phrases that we should keep in mind along with praying in Jesus' name, with faith, is . . .
   a. praying according to His will
   b. praying in the morning
   c. praying in unison
   d. praying in the same place
8. If evil men know how to give good gifts to their children, how much more will God give His children who ask the gift of . . .
   a. wisdom
   b. peace
   c. material blessings
   d. the Holy Spirit
9. The Lord promised Paul that just as he had testified before governors and kings and rulers in Jerusalem, he would also testify in . . .
   a. Ephesus
   b. Corinth
   c. Rome
   d. Philippi
10. Do you have a need for which God has a promise? And are you trusting God's promises to meet that need?
    a. I haven't thought about it
    b. I haven't trusted God's promises
    c. I want to trust God's promises
    d. I will trust God's promises

CHAPTER IV

Examples of Prayer

From the Bible

The greatest examples of prayer come from the Holy Scriptures. For God has placed them there to instruct us, to encourage us, and to assure us that He sees and hears and knows and cares, and that He responds to our prayers.

Jesus

The greatest example of all in prayer is Jesus. He went out early to pray. He spent nights in prayer (Luke 6:12). It was in the garden where he was praying that He was arrested.

His disciples were so impressed with His praying that they came to Him and requested, "Lord, teach us to pray" (Luke 11:1).

Before His death for us He prayed the great priestly prayer recorded in John 17. Study this entire chapter. In this prayer Jesus said, "I pray for them . . . which thou hast given me; for they are thine. . . . keep [them] through thine own name. . . . I pray not that thou shouldest take them out of the world, but that thou shouldest keep them from the evil. . . . As thou hast sent me into the world, even so have I also sent them into the world. . . . Neither pray I for these alone, but for them also which shall believe on me through their word. . . . Father, I will that they also, whom thou hast given me, be with me where I am; that they may behold my glory, which thou hast given me: for thou lovedst me before the foundation of the world."

His prayer in the Garden of Gethsemane on the night of His arrest was "not my will, but thine, be done" (Luke 22:42).

His prayers on the Cross were, "Father, forgive them; for they know not what they do" (Luke 23:24) and "Father, into thy hands I commend my spirit" (v. 46).

And His last words to His disciples, before His ascension, were a promise that He would send the promise to the Father, the Holy Spirit, upon them if they would tarry (pray and wait) in the city of Jerusalem. He promised that they would "be endued with power from on high" (Luke 24:49).

His last words were a promise that He would answer their patient expectant prayer.

From the Old Testament—PRAYERS OF DAVID

These are prayer portions taken from Psalms 4-18.

Hear me when I call, O God of my righteousness: thou hast enlarged me when I was in distress; have mercy upon me, and hear my prayer (4:1).

Give ear to my words, O LORD, consider my meditation. Hearken unto the voice of my cry, my King, and my God: for unto thee will I pray. My voice shalt thou hear in the morning, O LORD; in the morning will I direct my prayer unto thee, and will look up. . . .

But as for me, I will come into thy house in the multitude of thy mercy: and in thy fear will I worship toward thy holy temple. . . .

But let all those that put their trust in thee rejoice: let them ever shout for joy, because thou defendest them: let them also that love thy name be joyful in thee (5:1-3, 7, 11).

Have mercy upon me, O LORD; for I am weak: O LORD, heal me; for my bones are vexed. My soul is also sore vexed: but thou, O LORD, how long? Return, O LORD, deliver my soul: oh save me for thy mercies' sake. . . .

The LORD hath heard my supplication; the LORD will receive my prayer (6:2-4, 9).

I will praise thee, O LORD, with my whole heart; I will shew forth all thy marvellous works. I will be glad and rejoice in thee: I will sing praise to thy name, O thou most High. . . .

And they that know thy name will put their trust in thee: for thou, LORD, hast not forsaken them that seek thee (9:1, 2, 10).

Hear the right, O LORD, attend unto my cry, give ear unto my prayer, that goeth not out of feigned lips. . . .

Thou hast proved mine heart; thou has visited me in the night; thou hast tried me, and shalt find nothing; I am purposed that my mouth shall not transgress. . . .

Shew thy marvellous loving-kindness, O thou that savest by thy right hand them which put their trust in thee from those that rise up against them. Keep me as the apple of the eye, hide me under the shadow of thy wings. From the wicked that oppress me, from my deadly enemies, who compass me about (17:1, 3, 7-9).

I will love thee, O LORD, my strength. . . .

I will call upon the LORD, who is worthy to be praised: so shall I be saved from mine enemies. The sorrows of death compassed me, and the floods of ungodly men made me afraid. The sorrows of hell compassed me about: the snares of death prevented me (18:1, 3-6).

In my distress I called upon the Lord, and cried unto my god: he heard my voice out of his temple, and my cry came before him, even into his ears. . . .

He sent from above, he took me, he drew me out of many waters. He delivered me from my strong enemy, and from them which hated me: for they were too strong for me. . . .

He brought me forth also into a large place; he delivered me, because he delighted in me. The LORD rewarded me according to my righteousness; according to the cleanness of my hands hath he recompensed me. For I have kept the ways of the LORD, and have not wickedly departed from my God. . . .

For thou wilt light my candle: the LORD my God will enlighten my darkness. . . .

The LORD liveth; and blessed be my rock; and let the God of my salvation be exalted. It is God that avengeth me, and subdueth the people under me. He delivereth me from mine enemies: yea, thou liftest me up above those that rise up against me: thou hast delivered me from the violent man. Therefore will I give thanks unto thee, O LORD, among the heathen, and sing praises unto thy name (18:1, 3-6, 16, 17, 19-21, 28, 46-49).

These examples help us to know how to pray and what to pray for. For additional examples of some answered Bible prayers read about Abram's prayer for an heir in Genesis 15:2-6; about Eliezer's prayer to find a wife for Isaac in Genesis 24:12-26; about Moses stopping the plagues in Exodus chapters 8 through 10. Read about Gideon's fleece (Judges 6), and Elijah's prayer for the widow's son to be revived (1 Kings 17:21, 22). The raising of Lazarus can be found in John 11; the release of Peter from prison, Acts 12; the results of the prayers of Cornelius in Acts 10.

All of these should increase our faith and cause us to pray.

UNDERSTANDING WHAT YOU READ

NOTE: Recall or find these answers from the paragraphs you have just read. You may want to write your answers on a separate piece of paper so as not to mark your book.

In this section we have looked at examples of prayer from Jesus and David—from the New and Old Testaments.

1. The Great Priestly Prayer of Jesus is found in _____.
2. In the Garden of Gethsemane, Jesus prayed "_____."
3. On the Cross Jesus prayed "Father _____ them."
4. Many prayers of David are recorded in _____.

Answers on page 135.

From Our Family

The Reverend J. H. Walker, Sr., my father-in-law, was for nine years the general overseer of the Church of God. During his ministry from youth until his death at age seventy-six, his life was filled with testimonies of God's response to his prayers.

When he first felt impressed that he should go to Bible school he had to overcome many oppositions of the enemy. He was offered a promotion in his job and part ownership in the furniture business.

He went out collecting accounts owed the business to get everything in order before leaving, and somehow lost the roll of money collected. It took the cash from the sale of his piece of land to pay that back and left him no funds for school.

On the day the community was giving him a farewell party, with a broken heart he was preparing to tell them he would not be able to go to Bible school. But at the farewell gathering was the Western Union clerk who delivered him a letter that had just arrived, and in that letter was the offer of a music teaching position at the school. He could earn his keep. He would be able to go.

Later, when he was Superintendent of Education (1934), his

appendix ruptured. "I'm sorry, Professor, but it is too late now. There is nothing that can be done," the doctor reported.

But some of the leaders of the church—E. M. Ellis, M. P. Cross, T. L. McLain, and others—came in to pray for him. As they prayed, Brother Walker reported later, "I ceased to hear them; and a while later . . . I saw, as it were, a white, silvery velvet sheet floating down from the top of the room; and as it settled on my bed, I saw what appeared to be a long sword, shining like a neon tube. It came down and pierced my side. My body trembled like a leaf in the wind. I felt the heavenly anointing. I felt rested, and a sweet peace thrilled me, as I said, 'I'm healed. God has healed me!' . . . Praise God, I was healed." (From *When You Pray*, p. 150.)

Not long ago Brother Walker's wife, Blanche Jinkerson Walker, shared with me another special answer to prayer. She and Brother Walker were living in Dallas, Texas, and pastoring the Oak Cliff Church. It was time for annual income taxes to be paid. They had saved and planned and prayed and were still short $200 the day before the taxes were due.

Finally Brother Walker decided that it might be necessary to go to the bank and try to borrow the money. They drove to the bank, pulled into the parking area, but Brother Walker delayed to go in. He started praying again—"God you could do this for me. You could help us if You would." Then he decided to go back home and give God a little more time.

When they arrived home, the Walkers got on their knees and were calling again on the Lord for his help, when a knock was heard at the door. Sister Walker went to the door. There she saw a man who held out to her an envelope saying, "I brought this to you." Inside was the exact amount—$200.

Neither of the Walkers knew who the man was nor the reason for bringing the money. They never saw him again.

To them he was the angel of the Lord making a delivery.

From Our Children

My daughter, Crystal, is a missionary in Taiwan. When she first went to Taiwan she was alone at a language school where she was trying to learn Chinese.

One night she was awakened by a mighty blow against her dorm door. It seemed to be the intent of someone to break down the door and come in.

Crystal jumped from her bed, calling on the Lord, and started over toward the door.

"He will not get in," the Lord emphatically stated. "He will not get in!" The message was so clear that Crystal moved back toward her bed and, although there were more blows, the door held.

Later Crystal learned that an expert in martial arts had been the one attempting to knock the door down.

Ordinarily he would have easily succeeded. A girlfriend of his had formerly occupied that room and he must have thought she still lived there.

But God kept the door shut. God protected His child within.

Dianne's experience is an example of the listening prayer. My daughter, Dianne, was in the process of completing her dissertation and defending it for a Ph.D. in Counseling Psychology. As she was busy in the kitchen, she heard the Lord say, "Dianne, go into the living room and sit down; I want to talk with you."

She went into the living room and sat down to hear what the Lord had to say and He said, "Something is going to happen that you do not expect. But you are not to be afraid. You are not to panic. I am in control." God did not tell her what it was, He only prepared her to be strong and to put her trust in Him. He directed her to read 2 Chronicles 20, which teaches that "the battle is the Lord's."

The next day, the telephone rang and Dianne was told that her major professor, the head of the department, had been sent to the hospital very ill. This would mean that he would not be present for the defense of her dissertation, her final oral examination in securing her doctorate.

This professor had been very supportive of Dianne throughout her program, and naturally she felt shaken at losing him from her committee at this critical time. But God loved her and understood this, and prepared her not only for her own need but also she had the assurance that God knew what was happening to her professor.

Her professor survived the illness, and God saw Dianne through the successful defense of her dissertation.

How good God is in times when we need Him most.

EXAMPLES OF PRAYER 49

UNDERSTANDING WHAT YOU READ

In this section we have read personal examples of prayer experiences.
1. When J. H. Walker, Sr., suffered a ruptured appendix and was not expected to live, during a prayer God _____.
2. When Crystal's safety was threatened by someone attempting to break down her door, God _____ _____.
3. When Dianne might have panicked at the unexpected change of events, God _____ and _____.

Answers on page 135.

From Friends

The Reverend Edwin and Doris Tull were for many years tremendous blessings to the Lee College campus. Edwin was campus pastor and counselor. Doris was one of the librarians and kept flowers and fudge on her desk for all to enjoy.

Both of them shared marvelous experiences of answered prayer throughout their years of ministry.

Doris shared one special experience when they drove off to go to their first pastorate in Maine. All their belongings were in the car. It was a stormy night as they drove toward their destination. Suddenly the road divided but there was no sign to indicate where each led. "If we take the wrong road we could get caught in a blizzard with no gas stations, no homes nearby. We must pray and ask the Lord to help us know which road to take," Doris advised.

As they prayed Doris said a beautiful limousine drove up beside them, a chauffeur, in a uniform with brass buttons, got out in the rain, walked in front of their car, bowed and indicated with his hand the road they were to take.

Before they could speak to him, the chauffeur and car were gone. Doris and Edwin took the road pointed out to them, and before long came upon a sign that let them know they were headed in the right direction.

"Edwin," Doris commented, after some thought, "we didn't even tell him where we wanted to go."

Later, while in Maine, the Tulls were living on meager fare. Their work was pioneer, hard, very little income, rough surroundings, poor accommodations. One day as Edwin was talking with the Lord, he just mentioned casually that it would be nice to have a piece of candy, and some to share with his family.

In a short while there was an unexpected knock at the door. Seldom did they have visitors. What a surprise to find the general overseer standing there. He was wearing a long dark overcoat with large pockets. What a second surprise when J. H. Walker, the overseer, pulled out of his pocket a large sack of candy and handed it to Edwin Tull.

"Just think," Edwin said, "God not only sent me a sack of candy but he sent it by my beloved general overseer."

Together they had a good cry about the love and tenderness of Jesus and His response to His children's requests.

From Another Friend, in Germany

I wish to include this experience as it was reported in the European Action Report, Vol. 7, No. 2. It is an experience of Dieter Wagner.

> For some time I had felt a need for more of God's blessing in my ministry. It was July, 1982, vacation time, and my family and I were visiting with my wife's parents in the Stuttgart area. I decided to take off on my own to seek the Lord in prayer and fasting and intensive Bible study.
>
> Saying goodbye to the family, I got into the car and headed towards the Pfalz Forest, near the French border. I hadn't been driving very long when the Lord clearly spoke to me. Instead of turning off at the desired exit, I was to drive to the next parking area. I obeyed, wondering what on earth was going to happen.
>
> The parking area was near a lake, and when I saw the conglomeration of cars, and people lying around in the sun, my first impulse was to turn and leave. I had wanted to be alone for a while but it seemed the Lord had something for me to do first.
>
> I hadn't been there more than two minutes when a man and his wife approached me.
>
> "Are you a minister?" the man asked.

In my amazement I replied, "Well . . . yes, I am!"

"Do you believe in infant or adult baptism?" was his next question.

Quoting from the New Testament, I told him that only those persons who had repented of their sins and received Jesus as their Savior could be baptized. They seemed satisfied.

"What's the correct form of baptism, sprinkling or immersion? they then wanted to know.

Again, I showed them what the Bible says.

"Our church only believes in infant baptism and we haven't been baptized since becoming Christians," they went on to explain.

As we talked, I learned that God had told the husband to drive to this parking area, where he would meet a person who would answer his questions. After looking at some more Bible verses, they said, "There's water here, is there anything to stop us being baptized?"

After asking them if they believed in Jesus as the Son of God and making sure that they were Christians, I went into the water with them and baptized them in the name of the Father, Son, and Holy Spirit. When we got out of the water, they looked at me with glowing faces.

"I'm a worker in my church," the man said. "And I know it's not going to be easy to explain this truth to the others."

I encouraged him to stand on the Bible as God's Word and ask the Lord for wisdom, courage, and strength. After committing them to the Lord in prayer, I got into my car, turned out of the parking area and headed down the autobahn, marveling at the leading of the Lord. I'm proving that if we really mean business with Him, He will use us in the most amazing ways.

UNDERSTANDING WHAT YOU READ

In this section you have read of only two families and their experiences in prayer. The world is full of parallel testimonies.

1. When the Tulls did not know which road to take, in answer to prayer, God _____.
2. When Dieter Wagner made an appointment to seek the Lord, the Lord made an _____ for Dieter.
3. God brought _____ and a praying couple together in Europe, as he brought Cornelius and _____ together in Asia (Acts 10), and Philip and the eunuch together (Acts 8).

Answers on page 135.

FOR FURTHER STUDY

Walker, Lucille. *When You Pray.* Cleveland: Pathway Press, 1983.

Haden, Ben. *Pray.* Nashville: Thomas Nelson Publishers, 1974.

SELF-CHECK TEST

Answer the following questions without looking at the text of chapter four. When you finish, grade yourself from the answers on page 138. If you get eight or more correct, proceed to the next chapter. If you miss three or more, you should read the chapter again, retake the test, and then go on to chapter five.

Circle the letter of the response which you believe to be correct.

Circle T if true and F if false.

T F 1. The greatest examples of prayer come from the Holy Scriptures.

T F 2. Jesus is our greatest example in prayer.

T F 3. In His priestly prayer (John 17), Jesus prayed only for the disciples who were present with Him.

T F 4. The last words of Jesus before his ascension were a promise to send the Holy Spirit upon His waiting, praying disciples.

T F 5. King David prayed, "I will call upon the Lord, who is worthy to be praised; so shall I be saved from my enemies."

T F 6. Eliezer's prayer for a wife for Isaac was immediately answered.

T F 7. When the church prayed for Peter who was in prison, they were not surprised at his release.

T F 8. The Reverend J. H. Walker, Sr., testifies of being healed of a ruptured appendix.

T F 9. The Reverend and Mrs. Edwin Tull testify that God gave them direction when they did not know which way to go.

T F 10. Dieter Wagner testifies that God arranged a divine appointment for him on the European autobahn (interstate highway).

CHAPTER V

How, When, and Where to Pray

How Should We Pray?

R. A. Torrey wrote an entire book entitled *How to Pray,* and many other writers offer steps and suggestions on how to pray.

The Lord's Prayer

Perhaps the best place to start to learn how to pray is to look more carefully at the prayer that Jesus taught us to pray. We call it the Lord's Prayer and it is recorded in Matthew 6 and Luke 11.

As you analyze the Lord's Prayer you find that it begins with God as our Father. We recognize that He is high and holy and His name is hallowed. He is King of a kingdom where His will is done. And our first prayer request is that his kingdom will come to this earth, within us, and that His will may be done in earth, in us, as it is in heaven.

It is a prayer of relationships between God and one who is praying. There is the relationship of Father and child, of King and subject, of Master and servant, of Benefactor and beneficiary, of Guide and pilgrim.

Also you will observe that one cannot pray selfishly and pray the Lord's prayer. We must bring others into our prayers. We are to pray *our* Father, give *us* daily bread; forgive *us our* debts, as *we* forgive; lead *us* not into temptation; deliver *us* from evil. There are no single *I's* in the Lord's Prayer—no *me* or *my's*—only *we* and *us* and *our.*

It is all right to ask. We ask for His kingdom to come, His will to be done, for our daily food, for forgiveness of sins, and assistance in our forgiveness of others. We ask for victory over temptations and deliverance from Satan, the evil one.

Then we conclude by praising God for His kingdom and His power and we give Him glory that is due Him forever.

UNDERSTANDING WHAT YOU READ

NOTE: Recall or find these answers from the paragraphs you have just read.

In this section we have looked at how to pray using the Lord's Prayer as a model.

1. Jesus began His prayer by using the words of address "_____."
2. Here, as in the Garden, the basis of His petition was, "not my _____ but _____ be done."
3. Jesus taught us to pray to be delivered from _____.

Answers on page 135.

Contents

In a book *The Hour That Changes the World,* the author, Dick Eastman, suggests a prayer circle or wheel that has 12 segments or spokes. I find this to be a workable, effective guide to an hour of prayer or more. (1) He begins with entering into God's presence with praise, recognizing God's nature (Psalm 63:3); (2) Waiting in silent soul surrender to God (Psalm 46:10); (3) Confessing our need of God, our love of God, and our desire to please Him (Psalm 139:23); (4) Praying Scripture, reading the Word and praying the Word (Jeremiah 23:29); (5) Watching, developing holy alertness (Colossians 4:2); (6) Intercession, praying for others, for the world, for rulers (1 Timothy 2:1, 2); (7) Petition, sharing our own personal needs (Matthew 7:7); (8) Thanksgiving, counting our blessings (1 Thessalonians 5:18); (9) Singing to God, worshiping in hymns and spiritual songs (Psalm 100:2); (10) Meditating, pondering what God is saying to us (Joshua 1:8); (11) Listening, receiving spiritual instruction (Ecclesiastes 5:2); (12) Back to praise again, beginning and ending with the greatness and goodness of God (Psalm 52:9).

ACTS For shorter times of prayer someone has come up with the simple acrostic ACTS: A—Adoration, recognition, and worship of God. C—Confession, preparation of our heart. T—Thanksgiving, praise for what God has done, is doing, and will do. S—Supplication, making our needs and the needs of others known.

UNDERSTANDING WHAT YOU READ

In this section we have looked at elements that might be included in our prayers.

1. In the prayer circle, the author begins and ends with _____.
2. Time was also included for S_____ and L_____.
3. ACTS stands for A_____ C_____ T_____ S_____.

Answers on page 136.

Position

Prayer can be alone or with others. Prayer can be private or public. Each person needs to develop an entire life of prayer. Particularly does each person need his own individual quiet time each day with God. Also, there are many values of praying in groups. Group prayer is one of the highest expressions of fellowship, of unity, of moving us out of self toward the needs and burdens of others.

One can pray in any position; including kneeling (Psalm 95:6), standing (Mark 11:25), falling on one's face (Numbers 16:22; Matthew 26:39), with uplifted hands (Psalm 28:2), with eyes uplifted (Psalm 121:1), lying in bed (Psalm 63:6), and walking (Genesis 5:24).

Voice

We can sit in silent adoration; we can use conversational words; we can read the Psalms aloud, sing our prayers and praises, dance before Him as David did, pray aloud, pray in tongues, shout our prayers and praises, whisper them, or think them.

Attitude

Our attitude is more important than our position. We should pray in faith, in humility, in reverence, keeping His commandments, praying in His name, according to his will, with thanksgiving, surrendering ourselves to the Lord, seeking to know Him and to please Him, accompanied by an attitude of obedience and service.

The discussion concerning how to pray could go on and on. See the books suggested under *For Further Study*.

To conclude I would like to mention the Six S method suggested by Evelyn Christenson in *What Happens When Women Pray*. She suggests (1) one **S**ubject at a time; (2) one or two **S**entences; (3) **S**imple prayers in everyday vocabulary; (4) **S**pecific requests; (5) **S**ilent periods of listening; and (6) **S**mall groups.

UNDERSTANDING WHAT YOU READ

In these sections we considered position, voice, and attitude.
1. Name at least four positions one can use when praying _____, _____, _____.
2. One can pray with or without _____.
3. We should pray in the name of _____.
Answers on page 136.

The Example of Jesus

Again we look to Jesus to consider the time to pray. In Mark 1:35 we read that "rising up a great while before day, he went out, and departed into a solitary place, and there prayed." In Luke 6:12 we read that "he went out into a mountain to pray, and continued all night in prayer to God."

Jesus prayed before the great events of His life: before choosing the Twelve, when the people wanted to make Him king, when they plotted to kill Him. When life was especially busy, He withdrew for prayer.

Jesus was in constant communion with God. Our whole life too should be a life of constant communion with God and in constant meditation on His Word.

Bible Times

"Evening and morning, and at noon, will I pray, and cry aloud: and he shall hear my voice," declares the psalmist (55:17).

The Bible records that in his chamber Daniel "kneeled upon his knees three times a day, and prayed, and gave thanks before his God" (Daniel 6:10).

When we are suffering, sick, or sinful we are told to pray (James 5:13-16).

Paul advises us to pray "always" (Ephesians 6:18) and to "pray without ceasing" (1 Thessalonians 5:17).

In other words, we should stay in constant touch with God, living always in the awareness of His presence. Brother Lawrence wrote a classic entitled *The Practice of the Presence of God*. He says that our only business is to love and delight ourselves in God, and that we should establish ourselves in a sense of God's presence by continually conversing with Him. He believed that we should perform all of our actions for the love of God. His prayer was a sense of the presence of God with him continually.

Set Times

Even though we try to live always in an attitude of prayer and an awareness of God's presence, still we also need to have regular, specified prayer times—like Daniel and David.

It is good to *begin* the day with God when we get our bearings, offer to Him the day, commit ourselves to Him, look into His Word, listen to what He has to say to us, and feed our soul.

It is good also to *end* the day with God when we evaluate the day, give thanks for God's help, lay to rest the cares of the day, take hold of His peace, and commit ourselves to His protection through the night.

These times should not be left to chance, but should be isolated from distractions, committed to Him in adoration, confession, petition, intercession, thanksgiving, reading His Word, meditation, and praising.

UNDERSTANDING WHAT YOU READ

In this section we considered when to pray.
1. The psalmist said he prayed _____.
2. The New Testament says we should live in a constant attitude of prayer. Paul put it this way in 1 Thessalonians 5:17 "_____."

Answers on page 136.

One writer said that the *best* time, not the leftover time should be given to the Lord. Our daily prayer time should become a regular part of our schedule. Choose a reasonable length of time and stick to it. Begin with 15 minutes a day, then you can extend it as you grow in prayer. Jesus asked, "Could you not watch with me one hour?" That would be a worthy goal to set.

Where to Pray

Where is as important as when and how long—because although it too is flexible in that you can and should pray anywhere and everywhere, still you need a special place of prayer.

You need a private place, uninterrupted, where you can pray and sing aloud. Jesus went to a solitary place; He went into the mountains, into the desert. Jesus refers to your quiet place as entering "into thy closet, and when thou hast shut thy door, pray to thy Father which is in secret; and thy Father which seeth in secret shall reward thee openly" (Matthew 6:6).

A poor woman in a great city, never able to free herself from the insistent clamor of her little ones, made for herself a sanctuary in the simplest way. "I threw my apron over my head," she said, "and there was my closet."

A man who was having a similar problem said, "I just cover my face with my hat, and I am as much alone with God as in a closet."

The songwriter wrote:
> Take time to be holy,
> The world rushes on;
> Spend much time in secret
> With Jesus alone:
> By looking to Jesus
> Like Him thou shalt be;
> Thy friends in thy conduct
> His likeness shall see
> ("Take Time to be Holy" by W. D. Longstaff,
> *Hymns of the Spirit*, p. 273).

Someone reminds: Once you find the quiet place, don't forget the quiet heart.

UNDERSTANDING WHAT YOU READ

In this section we considered where to pray.

1. It is good to have a private place to pray where you will not be _____.
2. Jesus called our private place of prayer our _____.
3. One woman made herself a closet during the busy day by _____.

Answers on page 136.

FOR FURTHER STUDY

Eastman, Dick. *The Hour That Changes the World*. Grand Rapids: Baker Book House, 1978.

Christenson, Evelyn. *What Happens When Women Pray*. Wheaton: Scripture Press Publications, 1980.

Torrey, R. A. *How to Pray*. Chicago: Moody Press.

SELF-CHECK TEST

Answer the following questions without looking at the text of chapter five. When you finish, grade yourself from the answers on page 139. If you get eight or more answers correct, proceed to the next chapter. If you miss three or more, you should read the chapter again, retake the test, and then go on to chapter six.

True-False

Circle T if the answer is true and circle F if the answer is false.

T F 1. "The Lord's Prayer" is recorded in John 17.

T F 2. One cannot pray self-centeredly while praying the Lord's Prayer.

T F 3. Intercessory prayer is prayer for others.

T F 4. ACTS is an acrostic that sets forth a simple pattern for prayer.

T F 5. It is better to kneel than stand while praying.

T F 6. Our attitude in prayer is more important than our words or our position.

T F 7. Evelyn Christenson proposes the Six S method of prayer.

T F 8. Jesus prayed three times a day.

T F 9. Daniel prayed three times a day.

T F 10. One can make a prayer "closet" almost anywhere if it is necessary.

CHAPTER VI

Hindrances to Prayer

Satan hinders. We know that Satan desires to hinder our prayers. He first tries to keep us from praying. Then he causes us to doubt or to give up before the answer comes. And from the Book of Daniel we are shown that demonic forces actually do battle with the angels of God in their ministry to us.

We Christians do not need to focus on Satan but we do not need to shut our eyes and pretend He is not there. There are two kingdoms at war in our world, the kingdom of darkness and the kingdom of light, the kingdom of Satan and the kingdom of God. We are engaged in spiritual warfare (Ephesians 6). Satan and his evil powers are in rebellion against God. The devil is our enemy. Jesus came "that through death he might destroy him that had the power of death, that is, the devil" (Hebrews 2:14). For three weeks Daniel had fasted and prayed, asking God for understanding of the end-time vision which he had received. Then in Daniel 10:10-14 the answer came:

> And behold, an hand touched me, which set me upon my knees and upon the palms of my hands. And he said unto me, O Daniel, a man greatly beloved, understand the words that I speak unto thee, and stand upright: for unto thee am I now sent. And when he had spoken this word unto me, I stood trembling.
> Then he said unto me, Fear not, Daniel: for from the first day that thou didst set thine heart to understand, and to chasten thyself before thy God, thy words were heard, and I am come for thy words.
> But the prince of the kingdom of Persia withstood me one and twenty days: but, lo, Michael, one of the chief princes, came to help me; and I remained there with the kings of Persia.
> Now I am come to make thee understand what shall befall thy people in the latter days: for yet the vision is for many days.

The children of God need to know that Jesus has defeated Satan and that through Jesus we are able to rebuke him and command him and his powers to leave us. James reminds us: "Submit yourselves therefore to God. Resist the devil, and he will flee from you" (4:7). Jesus showed us how to overcome Satan when He was attacked by him following His baptism. Jesus quoted the Word of God, stood on the Word, and said, "Get thee behind me, Satan." See the temptation of Christ in Luke 4.

Merrill F. Unger in *Biblical Demonology* points out, "To repair the damage instigated and wrought by Satan, the Logos, the image of the invisible God, left the bosom of the Father (John 1:1, 14), took upon Himself humanity (Philippians 2:5-7), and wrought redemption, not only for men's salvation (Colossians 1:14; 2 Corinthians 5:21), but for the earth's deliverance as well (Matthew 13:44; Ephesians 1:14; Revelation 5:1-10). Therefore, Satan and the demons tried, in every possible way, to tempt or to kill Christ, in order that there might not be the shedding of blood, according to the Scriptures (Matthew 2:16; 4:1-11; Luke 4:29; 22:3, 44). The *same intense opposition*, shown against Christ, *is manifested* against *all believers* united to Him, and who are one 'in Him' (Ephesians 6:10, 12). . . . *salvation* and *safety are to be found only in the blood of Jesus* (Revelation 12:11). Temporal and eternal ruin must inevitably be the portion of all who do not avail themselves of the divinely provided way of escape (Revelation 20:15).

"Victory over all the power of the evil one is not by human works or self-effort but on the basis of the believer's faith in his position in Christ." We are to be strong in the Lord and stand in the victory of Calvary. God has provided us a defensive armor (Ephesians 6:13) which we are to wear while praying constantly in the Spirit (6:18-20).

Only through this prayer at all seasons for all saints, with all perseverance and supplication, in the Spirit can we make use of the *strength which is in the Lord*. Through prayer the foe is vanquished and the victory is won.

Unger says that just as the physical body needs fresh air, pure water, sunlight, nourishing food, proper exercise, and general cleanliness for health; so the spirit needs an atmosphere of prayer, the food of the Word of God, the water of the Holy Spirit, walking in the light of Christ, to be engaged in spiritual service and separated from the evil of the world.

Just as the first provides the protection against the physical diseases, so the second provides immunity for the soul against demonic danger. "Every sinful act or neglect is a direct invitation to Satan and demons to gain a foothold, and work harm to the human soul." We must not be "ignorant of his devices" (2 Corinthians 2:11).

"But thanks be to God, which giveth us the victory through our Lord Jesus Christ" (1 Corinthians 15:57; 2 Corinthians 2:14; Romans 6:11).

UNDERSTANDING WHAT YOU READ

NOTE: Recall or find these answers from the paragraphs you have just read. You may want to write your answers on a separate piece of paper so as not to mark your book.

In this section we have studied how Satan seeks to hinder our praying.

1. The ruler of the kingdom of evil is _____.
2. The leader of the kingdom of God is our Captain _____.
3. Satan was defeated by Jesus at _____.
4. We overcome Satan by the _____ of Jesus.
5. We fight our battles by the Word, the Holy Spirit, the name of Jesus in _____.

Answers on page 136.

Ourselves

We have looked at Satan as one who hinders our prayers, but *we ourselves are guilty* in a multitude of ways *of causing hindrances* in getting our prayers through to God and receiving His answers.

I will briefly list and give biblical references to some of the ways we ourselves hinder prayer.

1. We pray with a selfish purpose. **We ask amiss** and not according to His will. "Ye ask, and receive not, because ye ask amiss, that ye may consume it upon your lusts" (James 4:3).
2. **Unbelief.** We don't ask in faith. We don't ask specifically and often would not recognize the answer or would be surprised if it came. "But let him ask in faith, nothing wavering. For he that wavereth is like a wave of the sea driven with the wind and tossed. For let not that man think that he shall receive any thing of the Lord" (James 1:6, 7).
3. **Neglect.** We fail to keep His commandments and do the things that please Him. "And whatsoever we ask, we receive of him, because we keep his commandments, and do those things that are pleasing in his sight" (1 John 3:22).
4. **Sin.** We don't confess our need and repent of our wrongs. "But your iniquities have separated between you and your God, and your sins have hid his face from you, that he will not hear" (Isaiah 59:2).
5. **We don't forgive others.** He forgives us as we forgive others. "But if ye forgive not men their trespasses, neither will your Father forgive your trespasses" (Matthew 6:15).
6. **We don't ask.** We complain. We wish. We would like, but we don't get around to simply asking. "Ye have not, because ye ask not" (James 4:2).
7. **We doubt** and we give up before the answer comes. Paul tells us of Abraham, "He staggered not at the promise of God through unbelief; but was strong in faith, giving glory to God; And being fully persuaded that, what he had promised, he was able also to perform" (Romans 4:20, 21).
8. **We don't give thanks.** We are told to pray with thanksgiving. "Be careful for nothing; but in every thing by prayer and supplication with thanksgiving let your requests be made known unto God" (Philippians 4:6). I have heard messages by the Holy Spirit say, "Answers come on wings of praise; healing comes on wings of praise."

HINDRANCES TO PRAYER

9. **We don't share** prayer needs with others. There is power in united prayer. We should pray with and for one another. "Again, I say unto you, That if two of you shall agree on earth as touching any thing that they shall ask, it shall be done for them of my Father which is in heaven. For where two or three are gathered together in my name, there am I in the midst of them" (Matthew 18:19, 20). Sometimes our pride keeps us from sharing our needs with others.

10. **We ignore the poor** and fail to help them. "Whoso stoppeth his ears at the cry of the poor, he also shall cry himself, but shall not be heard" (Proverbs 21:13).

11. **Trouble in the home.** Wrong relationships can hinder prayer. "Likewise, ye husbands, dwell with them [your wives] according to knowledge, giving honour unto the wife, as unto the weaker vessel, and as being heirs together of the grace of life; that your prayers be not hindered" (1 Peter 3:7).

12. **Idols** in our heart. We put other things in first place in our priorities. "Son of man, these men have set up their idols in their heart, and put the stumbling block of their iniquity before their face: should I be enquired of at all by them?" (Ezekiel 14:3).

13. **Lack of reconciliation** with fellow Christians. "Therefore if thou bring thy gift to the altar, and there rememberest that thy brother hath ought against thee; Leave there thy gift before the altar, and go thy way; first be reconciled to thy brother, and then come and offer thy gift" (Matthew 5:23, 24).

14. Do not forget also God's timetable. **We try to rush** God. We are impatient. It takes time for the garden to produce a crop. It takes time for a baby to be born. Healing can also come one day at a time.

15. Sometimes we hinder prayer by **refusing to do our part.** What if Ananias had not gone to the street called Straight and inquired in the house of Jason for one called Saul of Tarsus who was praying (Acts 9)? What if Cornelius had not sent servants to Joppa to call for one Simon, whose surname is Peter (Acts 10)? And what if Peter had refused to go to the Gentile's home?

Have you felt God impressing you to speak to someone, visit someone, write a letter to someone? Did you obey?

UNDERSTANDING WHAT YOU READ

In this section we have looked at ways we may sometimes be guilty of causing hindrances to prayer.

1. We pray amiss when we ask for things to consume upon our own _____.
2. It is wrong to pray and not _____ that He will answer.
3. _____ will hide God's face from us so that He does not hear us.
4. If we do not forgive others, God will _____ _____ us.

Answers on page 136.

What to Do

What can we do when it seems that our prayers are not getting through? First, we can bind the powers of Satan in the name of Jesus and in the power of His blood. We can take authority over the hindrances of the enemy in the victory of Calvary.

Next, we can check out our own status before God. Have we asked according to His will? Have we asked others to join with us in prayer about our petitions? Are we praying with thanksgiving? Have we shut off our compassion for the poor? Are we praying with faith? Are we abiding in Him with clean hands and with forgiveness in our heart for others? Are we seeking Him rather than things from Him? Are we praying in the Spirit with a heart of love and a willingness to obey?

"Seek the Lord while he may be found, call ye upon him while he is near: Let the wicked forsake his way, and the unrighteous man his thoughts: and let him return unto the Lord, and he will have mercy upon him; and to our God, for he will abundantly pardon" (Isaiah 55:6, 7).

UNDERSTANDING WHAT YOU READ

In this section we have searched our heart by questioning if we are guilty of the hindrances and by asking what we can do about it.

1. Yes, I have _____ my own heart.
2. Yes, He will _____ pardon.
3. I will pray with _____ and with _____.

Answers on page 136.

FOR FURTHER STUDY

Lovett, C. S. *Dealing With the Devil.* Baldwin Park, CA: Personal Christianity, 1967.

Unger, Merrill F. *Biblical Demonology.* Wheaton: Scripture Press Publications, 1952.

SELF-CHECK TEST

Answer the following questions without looking at the text of chapter six. When you finish, grade yourself from the answers on page 139. If you get eight or more answers correct, proceed to the next chapter. If you miss three or more, you should read the chapter again, retake the test, and then go on to chapter seven.

Multiple Choice

Circle the letter before the response you believe to be correct.

1. The devil knows that we can accomplish more through our prayers than through our work. Therefore he . . .
   a. hinders our praying
   b. opposes our praying
   c. tries to keep us from praying
   d. all of the above

2. We, as followers of Jesus, have victory over the devil through . . .
    a. the Word of God
    b. the blood of Jesus
    c. prayer in Jesus' name
    d. all of the above
3. Some have not because . . .
    a. they ask not
    b. they believe not
    c. they praise not
    d. all of the above
4. Jesus teaches that if we want God to forgive us, we must . . .
    a. go to church
    b. read the Bible
    c. forgive others
    d. do penance
5. Sin separates us from God and hides His face from us. Therefore if we sin and we want God to forgive us, we must . . .
    a. make restitution
    b. crawl on our knees to the altar
    c. confess and repent
    d. punish ourselves
6. Praying with others is a good idea because Jesus promised that where two or three were gathered together in His name He would . . .
    a. be present
    b. make a record of it
    c. give them merit points
    d. send an angel
7. Praying with others is a good idea also because Jesus said that if two of you shall agree, be united, in what you are praying for, it shall be . . .
    a. considered
    b. placed on high priority
    c. hoped for
    d. done
8. The way we treat the poor has an effect on our success

in praying. Because God says that if we close our ears to the cry of the poor, we shall cry to Him but He will . . .
   a. be far away
   b. not hear us
   c. send someone else
   d. say, "come back tomorrow"
9. If it seems that our prayers are not getting through to God, we should . . .
   a. take authority over hindrances of Satan
   b. take inventory of our life
   c. confess our need of the Lord's help
   d. all of the above
10. Sometimes we hinder prayer because we do not do our part. We need to practice:
   a. instant expectations
   b. miraculous faith
   c. listening and obedience
   d. chanting our prayers

CHAPTER VII

How God Answers

God Answers

God does answer sincere prayer. The Word of God, which will endure even if heaven and earth pass away, declares that God hears and answers prayer. "Call unto me, and I will answer thee," God says in Jeremiah 33:3. And millions in the Bible and out have proved this to be true.

"The prayer of the upright is his delight," declares Proverbs 15:8. "O thou that hearest prayer, unto thee shall all flesh come" (Psalm 65:2). "For mine house shall be called an house of prayer for all people" (Isaiah 56:7).

How God Answers

We shall explore how God answers the prayers of the upright. Sometimes He says *yes;* sometimes He says *no;* sometimes He says *wait;* sometimes He sends unexpected answers. We have already observed some of His conditions in the chapter dealing with hindrances. In this chapter we will also look at what Huegel refers to as 10 rules or laws of successful praying.

Surprise or Unexpected Answers

Sometimes we are surprised by God's answer. One minister, for instance, prayed that someone from his church would enter foreign service for God, but when his daughter decided to become a missionary he put obstacles in her way to try to stop her. He was unwilling to pay the price of having his prayer answered God's way.

Remember that prayer is not for the purpose of manipulating God to work for us but for preparing ourselves to work with Him.

One of my favorite illustrations concerning how God may answer us is the story of Everett Howard, a veteran missionary to the Cape Verde Islands. Dr. James Dobson records Everett's experience in a Regal book, *Emotions: Can You Trust Them?*

When I was just a young boy I knew God was calling me, but I was confused. I didn't know just where or when or what He wanted me to do. . . . I went on through school and college [and even dental school]. I was still fighting and battling away, unsure of God's direction for my life.

One day I came to the point of a definite decision. . . . So I went into the little church where my dad was pastoring and locked the doors so I could be alone. I knelt down at the little altar and took out a piece of paper and a pencil and said, "Now this is going to be for life!"

I listed everything on that page. I filled it with promises of what I would do for God, including my willingness to be a missionary, and every possible alternative I could think of. I promised to sing in the choir. . . . tithe, and read the Bible and do all the things I thought God might want of me. I had a long list of promises and I really meant them.

When I had finished that well-written page, I signed my name at the bottom and laid it on the altar. There . . . I looked up and waited for "thunder and lightning" or some act of approval from the Lord. I thought I might experience what the Saint Paul did on the road to Damascus, or something equally dramatic. . . . But nothing happened. It was quiet, and I was so disappointed.

I couldn't understand it. . . . I took out my pencil again and tried to think about what I'd left out. But I couldn't remember anything else. I prayed again and told the Lord that I had put everything possible on that paper. Still nothing happened, though I waited and waited.

Then it came. I felt the voice of God speaking. . . . He didn't shout. . . . I just felt in my own soul a voice speak so clearly. It said, "Son, you're going about it wrong. I don't want a consecration like this. Just tear up the paper you've written."

I said, "All right, Lord". . . and wadded it up.

Then . . . God seemed to whisper again, "Son, I want you to take a blank piece of paper, sign your name on the bottom . . . and let Me fill it in."

"Oh, . . . that's different, Lord," I cried. But I did what He said.

It was just a secret between God and me, as I signed the paper. And God has been filling it in for the past 36 years.

Maybe I'm glad I didn't know what was going to be written on the page. Things like . . . lying sick in the lonely mountains of the Cape Verde Islands, burning up with fever . . . the famine, when almost a third of the population . . . starved to death . . . nine months without one single check or a penny . . . that wasn't written on the page until the time came. But, you know, there was no depression. Those were the most blessed days, because God was there! And if I could turn around and do it again, I'd go every step of the way that we've traveled for the last 36 years.

I hope you will also put your name at the bottom of a blank sheet of paper and let God fill it in. Especially if you're worried about who you should marry or where to go to school or what training you should get and all those questions. . . . You don't know the answers and neither do I. . . . But God knows. Let Him fill in the page. . . . And of this I am absolutely confident: the Lord will make His purposes and plans known in plenty of time for you to heed them.

UNDERSTANDING WHAT YOU READ

NOTE: Recall or find these answers from the paragraphs you have just read. You may want to write your answers on a separate piece of paper so as not to mark your book.

In this section we have introduced the proposition that God does answer prayer and have begun to consider how He answers.

1. God sometimes _____ us with the way He answers our prayer.
2. Four basic ways He answers are by saying _____, _____, or _____, or by sending _____.
3. God directed Everett Howard to sign an empty sheet of paper and let Him _____.
4. God answered the pastor's prayer for a missionary by _____.

Answers on page 136.

Our Way—God's Way

Ben Haden in his book, *Pray*, records a testimony of answered prayer found on the body of a Confederate soldier:

I asked for strength . . . that I might achieve.
He made me weak . . . that I might obey.

I asked for health . . . that I might do greater things.
I was given grace . . . that I might do better things.
I asked for riches . . . that I might be happy.
I was given poverty . . . that I might be wise.
I asked for power . . . that I might have the praise of men.
I was given weakness . . . that I might feel the need of God.
I asked for all things . . . that I might enjoy life.
I was given life . . . that I might enjoy all things.
I received nothing that I asked for
All that I hoped for.
My prayer was answered.

Another insight into our way of asking and God's desire to give us the right answer is clearly seen in a message by the Holy Spirit—a prophecy or interpretation of tongues—from a tape of F. J. May's Bible study at the 1975 Tennessee Camp Meeting. God said:

You have wanted glory; I have wanted you to be broken.
You have wanted fame; I have wanted humility.
You have wanted success; I wanted obedience and for you to carry your cross.
You have wanted power; I have wanted you to be filled with love.
I wanted you to be led; but you have not wanted to be guided.
I would have empowered you; but you would not obey.
HEAR ME NOW:
Cast your excuses aside and let me walk in your life. And I will take away the shame of your barrenness . . . and your coldness.
And I will touch you with holy flame and power, with the Holy Ghost and fire.
And ye shall be my witnesses in these last days, saith the Lord God Almighty.

UNDERSTANDING WHAT YOU READ

In this section we have looked at two contrasts of what we may ask for versus what God would desire for us to have or to be.

1. The words found on the Confederate soldier said that he was given weakness that he might feel the _____.
2. The Holy Spirit's message said, "You wanted power, but I wanted you to be filled with _____."
3. "Let me walk in your life," God pleads, "and I will touch you with holy flame and _____ and you shall be my _____ these last days."

Answers on page 136.

"No" Answers

We have declared that God always answers true prayer. Sometimes, however, He says *no*. Even the great Elijah got a *no* answer from God when he cried out, "O Lord, take away my life" (1 Kings 19:4). This same verse says, "He requested for himself that he might die."

God not only said no, but God performed several miracles in order to keep His prophet alive. He sent an angel with food and water to give him strength. In his time of depression God encouraged him. After the strong wind, earthquake, and fire, the Lord spoke with him in a small voice. The Lord encouraged Elijah and gave him a job to do. God sent him to anoint a new king over Syria, a new king over Israel, and to anoint Elisha to be Elijah's successor. God assured Elijah that he was not alone, that there were seven thousand faithful followers of Jehovah in Israel.

Have you ever gone through depression? Have you ever asked God to let you die? You may not have if you are young, but if you are older, you probably have been in circumstances of ill health, or tragedy, or family problems, or financial difficulties in which you have said, "O Lord, please let me die." I have.

But God has said no and come to our rescue and given us grace and strength and turned our sorrow into joy. That is part of His work on earth. Jesus read from Isaiah 61:1-3 when He returned to Nazareth after His baptism: "The Spirit of the Lord is upon me; because the Lord hath anointed me to preach good tidings unto the meek; he hath sent me to bind up the brokenhearted, to proclaim liberty to the captives, and the opening of the prison to them that are bound; To proclaim the acceptable year of the Lord, and the day of vengeance of our God; to comfort all that mourn; To appoint unto them that mourn in Zion, to give them beauty for ashes, the oil of joy for mourning, the garment of praise for the spirit of heaviness; that they might be called trees of righteousness, the planting of the Lord, that he might be glorified." And Jesus said that the Scripture was fulfilled in Him. So if we get discouraged, depressed, feel lonely or forsaken and we bring to Him ashes, mourning, and heaviness, His answers to us will be beauty, a garment of praise, and the oil of joy.

Let me just insert one warning here. We read that suicide is reaching epidemic proportions. Do not let yourself contemplate the ending of your life. That decision belongs to God. No matter how dark things may seem, remember Elijah. Tell God how you feel, and allow God to sustain your life. Do the work He gives you to do, and when it is finished He will take you home to be with Him. It will be worth it all when we see Jesus.

God not only said no to Elijah, He also said no to other good people. Jesus said no to Zebedee's wife when she requested Jesus to let her sons sit, one on the right hand and the other on the left, in His kingdom. Jesus said, "Ye know not what ye ask" (Matthew 20:22).

God also said no to the great Apostle Paul. He asked three times that his thorn in the flesh might depart from him (2 Corinthians 12:7, 8). But the Lord refused answering: "My grace is sufficient for thee: for my strength is made perfect in weakness" (v. 9). Paul's response was to accept God's answer as being for his good and Paul said, "Most gladly therefore will I rather glory in my infirmities, that the power of Christ may rest upon me" (v. 9). I wish we could always remember and believe the truth that "He gives the very best to those who leave the choice with Him."

> **UNDERSTANDING WHAT YOU READ**
>
> In this section we have seen that out of God's love for us He says no to some of our prayers.
> 1. The refusal to take away Paul's thorn in the flesh resulted in the perfection of God's _____ in Paul.
> 2. When Elijah got depressed and asked God to let him die, God kept him alive because God had more _____ for Elijah to do.
> 3. When God says no to us, it is because He _____ us.
>
> *Answers on page 136.*

"Yes" Answers

Rather than just give examples of *yes* answers, perhaps it would be more profitable to discuss some of the methods God uses to give us these answers. God answers prayer through the release of power within us, through the cooperation of others, and through direct creative action. Sometimes we hear the answer in our heart or with our mind. Sometimes God directs us to a Scripture passage that contains the answer. Other times He may influence our decisions. He may give us the answer as we listen to a sermon. He may send someone with the correct decision to us. He may use visions and dreams, tongues and interpretation or a word of knowledge, or a prophecy—the gifts of the Spirit. The true answer to prayer is the experience of God by our side—God with us.

Let me briefly cite just a few examples as to how He answers.

Nashville High School

I was a teacher in the Nashville City school system and had been filling in for a bookkeeping teacher who had had surgery. There was a great deal of ill-will between some of the students and some faculty members. Students had even hassled the teachers at their homes. The Lord gave me a message to the students and teachers—both were at fault. I meditated on it for sometime but procrastinated about asking the principal for an opportunity to speak. Then one Friday I received word that I would be transferred to another school the following week since the regular teacher was returning.

My spirit was grieved because I had not delivered God's message. It was Friday and we never had assembly on Friday. But I prayed, "O God, if You want this message delivered, have them announce assembly and I will ask to speak."

In just a short while a special called assembly was announced. I went immediately to the principal who was also a lay preacher, a sincere Christian. He gave me permission. Students and teachers shed tears. God touched their hearts. The result for me was great joy that I had obeyed the Lord.

At Sea

An old fisherman prayed every day that God would use him to help someone else. One day he was heading into the wind to go fishing when it suddenly occurred to him that there probably were as many fish with the wind as against the wind. "Why should I batter these waves," he thought. "Let us go with the wind." About an hour after he had changed course, he ran into four lifeboats with 14 men who had survived their ship that had burned. They had been praying for rescue.

The old fisherman believed that God had given him the idea to sail in the direction of the wind in order to answer the prayers of the 14 men.

Dr. Mary Ruth Morris Stone, former director of academic advising at Lee College, loves to tell the story of her great-grandfather who recovered his false teeth from the Chesapeake Bay. Frank Morris, her great-grandfather, was a man of faith and prayer. He prayed regularly three hours a day—an hour at dawn, an hour at noon, and an hour before retiring. One day while fishing, his false teeth fell out and dropped into the bay. Frank Morris went home that night and had a session with God about the need of his teeth. The next day he went out in his boat and on the first dip with his oyster tongs he retrieved his teeth.

When his son Bill told his dad that he was called to preach, Frank said, "I promise I will pray for your ministry one hour a day as long as I live."

This great-grandfather, now has one son, six grandchildren, six great-grandchildren, one great-great-grandson who are ministers and missionaries.

In Church

A friend of mine in Germany was sitting in church, meditating about something she felt the Lord was directing her to do. "Lord, I want to be sure that this is from You. If I know that You want me to do this, I will do it," she prayed. "Lord, if this is from You, let the preacher call my name." In just a short while, the minister referred to her by name in his message.

In the Military

Ronnie Hatcher was director of a servicemen's center in Europe and was having outstanding success in his ministry. But for some time there had been an unsettled feeling inside, a discontent that seemed to be challenging him to a change. While at a camp meeting he prayed, "O God, please let someone give me some clear direction. Use someone to tell me what You want me to do."

He had hardly finished the prayer when Dr. Cecil Knight walked into the room. Seeing Ronnie he walked straight to him and said, "Ronnie, you need to go to Northwest Bible College."

In Reading the Word

Several times the Lord has given me and members of our family answers through reading the Bible. Passages will *leap out*. Passages will become alive and will contain the answers we have been seeking. It may be in a passage being read. At times God directs to the exact book, chapter, and verse. There have been times when the Bible has fallen open to the place.

Let me cite one example: I became very disturbed that the ladies department of the denomination was not being treated equally with the other departments. In studying about it and praying about it, I felt that I should write a letter pointing out the inequities and requesting revision. While thinking about how to write the top leadership, I made it a matter of earnest prayer. "Lord, should I put this in writing?" I asked. Then God directed my attention, while I was on my knees, to a passage I was not even aware of.

There were the words: *"Shew the house to the house of Israel,* that they may be ashamed of their iniquities: and let them measure the pattern. And if they be ashamed of all that they have done, shew them the form of the house, and the fashion thereof . . . and *write it* in their sight, that they may keep the whole form thereof, and all the ordinances thereof, and do them. This *is the law of the house*; Upon the top of the mountain *the whole limit* thereof round *about shall be most holy.* Behold, this is the law of the house" (Ezekiel 43:10-12). I wrote the letter.

UNDERSTANDING WHAT YOU READ

In this section we have looked at examples of how God says yes when we pray.

1. Sometimes God gives us the answer in a passage of _____.

2. Sometimes we get the exact method we ask for as Ronnie did when someone walked in and said, "You need to _____."

Answers on page 136.

"Wait" or Delayed Answer

One of the best examples of the *wait* answer is Joseph. He knew from a child that God had a special purpose for His life. God gave Joseph dreams. But those very dreams brought the jealousy of his brothers and led to their selling him as a slave when he was seventeen. He was thirty years old when God delivered him from prison and set him up as a ruler in Egypt. Read the account in Genesis 37-41.

Perhaps the most difficult answer of all is the one that requires us to have patience, to keep on trusting and believing that we do have the answer.

Abraham is a prime example of waiting. God told him at the beginning of the covenant (See Genesis 15) that he would have a son from his own body that would be his heir and that his offspring would be as the stars in the heaven. The Bible says, "He [Abraham] believed in the Lord; and he counted it to him for righteousness" (15:6). But it was not until Abraham was one hundred years old that Isaac was born to Sarah. And that happened after Sarah had passed her child-bearing years (Genesis 21).

Ten Laws for Answered Prayer

F. J. Huegel in *Successful Praying* presents laws in the spiritual world that work just as do the laws of the natural world. We say objects fall because of the law of gravity, and heavy planes can fly because of the law of aerodynamics. In like manner, Huegel says there are laws which govern prayer. He calls them:

1. The Law of Atonement—the basis is the blood of Jesus and His victory at Calvary (Hebrews 10:19, 20).
2. The Law of Position—our place with Christ as believers (Ephesians 2:6).
3. The Law of Faith—which comes from hearing the Word (Mark 11:24).
4. The Law of Right Relations—we must also be right with our fellowman (Mark 11:25).
5. The Law of God's Will—He will hear if we ask according to His will (1 John 5:14).
6. The Law of the Spirit's Inspiration—the Spirit makes intercession for us (Romans 8:27).
7. The Law of Praise—God dwells in praise and praise brings victory (Psalm 22:3; Philippians 4:6).
8. The Law of Right Motive—we must seek God's glory (Romans 8:7, 8).
9. The Law of Right Diagnosis—we must pray from God's viewpoint; listen to God (Habakkuk 2:1).

10. The Law of Warfare—prayer must be aimed against God's foe—the devil (Colossians 2:15).

Enter into prayer in the authority of Christ's victory at Calvary, in your position as His child, by faith upon the Word of God, with a heart of forgiveness for your fellowman, asking in God's will, praying in the Spirit, praising God, with the desire to glorify God, listening to God's viewpoint, doing warfare against Satan—and *you will pray successfully.*

UNDERSTANDING WHAT YOU READ

In this section we looked at *wait* answers or delayed answers along with 10 "laws" of prayer proposed by Huegel.

1. Two outstanding examples of persons who waited in faith for the answer to be realized were _____ and _____.

2. Prayers are answered through the atonement by the _____ and _____ of Jesus in His victory over Satan.

3. The Law of the Spirit is effective because the Spirit prays according to _____ (read Romans 8:27).

4. The Law of Right Motive is effective because we are seeking _____.

5. In the Law of Warfare our prayer must be aimed against the enemy of God who is _____.

Answers on page 136.

FOR FURTHER STUDY

An Unknown Christian. *The Kneeling Christian.* Grand Rapids: Zondervan, 1971.

Haden, Ben, *Pray.* Nashville: Thomas Nelson Publishers, 1974.

Huegel, F. J. *Successful Praying.* Grand Rapids: Zondervan Publishing House, 1967.

SELF-CHECK TEST

After you have read chapter seven take this brief self-check listing test. Check answers on page 139.

List 7 of the 10 laws of successful praying. You may state them in your own words.

1. _____

2. _____

3. _____

4. _____

5. _____

6. _____

7. _____

List the 3 basic answers God gives along with surprise unexpected answers.

8. _____

9. _____

10. _____

CHAPTER VIII

What to Pray For

"For what may we pray?" asks McElroy in *Quiet Thoughts*. "Whatever is nearest and dearest to us, whatever weighs heaviest on our heart belongs in our prayers provided it is in accord with God's will." *The Living Bible* says in Philippians 4:6: "Don't worry about anything; instead, pray about everything; tell God your needs and don't forget to thank him for his answers."

Prayer is the expression of man's dependence on God for all things. Prayer is communion, praise, worship, thanksgiving, coming into His presence. It is also petition for ourselves and intercession for others. Particularly in this area of petition and intercession we need help in knowing how to pray.

We Need Help

The Bible recognizes that we need help and God has provided help for us when we pray. In Romans 8:26-28 we read: "The Spirit also helpeth our infirmities: for we know not what we should pray for as we ought: but the Spirit itself maketh intercession for us with groanings which cannot be uttered. And he that searcheth the hearts knoweth what is the mind of the Spirit, because he maketh intercession for the saints according to the will of God."

Good Models to Learn From

A good way to pray is to pray the Scriptures for they shall be fulfilled even if heaven and earth pass away. In praying the Scriptures we also can pray with confidence, for we know that we are praying with the mind and will of God.

Jesus, Our Highest Example

Let us briefly review in a short summary some of the things Jesus prayed for and taught us to pray for: He prayed for God's kingdom to come and His will to be done in the earth and in us. He said we should pray daily for bread, forgiveness, deliverance from temptation and from the Evil One. We should include praise and glory to the Father.

Jesus prayed for the healing of others. He prayed for their deliverance from evil spirits; He blessed the people; He wept over their lost condition. He prayed for unity. He prayed that they might know God and Jesus Christ whom God had sent. He prayed that they might have eternal life, that none of them should be lost (except the son of perdition that the Scriptures might be fulfilled). He prayed that they might have joy, be kept from the evil of the world, be sanctified through the Word, and that they might be with Him in heaven to share in His glory. These then are also good things for which we should pray.

UNDERSTANDING WHAT YOU READ

In this section we have looked at three things: What we should pray for, our need for help, and Jesus as model.

1. The Bible says that God has provided the _____ to help us when we pray.
2. The Spirit makes _____ for us according to the will of God.
3. Some of the things Jesus did in prayer were _____, _____, _____, _____.
4. When we say that Jesus is our model in prayer, this means that we should follow His _____.

Answers on page 136.

Old Testament Guides

Blessing—One of the beautiful prayers of the Old Testament that we should use is the blessing in Numbers 6:22-25: "The Lord spoke unto Moses, saying . . . On this wise ye shall bless the children of Israel, saying unto them, The Lord bless thee, and keep thee: The Lord make his face shine upon thee, and be gracious unto thee: The Lord lift up his countenance upon thee, and give thee peace."

I like to use this to bless others, and I like to pray it for myself: "O God, let Your face shine upon me; be gracious unto me; lift up Your countenance upon me and give me peace."

When separating—"The Lord watch between me and thee, when we are absent one from another" (Genesis 31:49).

On retiring—"I will both lay me down in peace, and sleep: for thou, Lord, only makest me dwell in safety" (Psalm 4:8).

Psalms—Most of the Psalms can be prayed. Especially beautiful and comforting is Psalm 23, "The Lord is my shepherd; I shall not want." Here are a few select lines of prayer from the Psalms. "Give ear to my words, O Lord . . . . Unto thee will I pray. My voice shalt thou hear in the morning (5:1-3). In thee do I put my trust (7:1). How excellent is thy name in all the earth (8:1). I will praise thee . . . with my whole heart (9:1). Have mercy upon me . . . for I am weak . . . heal me (6:2). I will call upon the Lord, who is worthy to be praised: so shall I be saved from mine enemies (18:3). One thing have I desired . . . [and] that will I seek after; that I may dwell in the house of the Lord all the days of my life, to behold the beauty of the Lord, and to enquire in his temple (27:4). Save me, O God (54:1). Be merciful unto me (26:11). Show me your ways, O Lord, teach me your paths . . . . you are God my Savior" (25:4, 5; *NIV*).

Nehemiah's prayers are an inspiration and a model. While in exile he heard that the wall of Jerusalem had been broken down and the gates burned with fire. "It came to pass, when I heard these words, that I sat down and wept, and mourned certain days, and fasted, and prayed before the God of heaven" (Nehemiah 1:4).

Read how Nehemiah confessed the sins of Israel to God, requested from the king that he might be able to go to Jerusalem and help rebuild the wall and the gates, and how with the help of the Lord he withstood opposition and succeeded in rebuilding the wall in 52 days.

The Bible instructs us to pray for nations and leaders. Blessings are promised on all who pray for the peace of Jerusalem. We are to pray for kings and those in authority that we may lead a quiet and peaceable life in all godliness and honesty. We are to pray that all people will come to know the Savior.

Solomon prayed for wisdom to lead the people of God. Joshua prayed for courage. Daniel prayed for the understanding of dreams and visions and the mysteries of God. Keep a notebook with your Bible and as you read make notes of the prayers throughout all the pages of the Bible.

UNDERSTANDING WHAT YOU READ

In this section we touched briefly on a few examples from the Old Testament as to what to pray for.

1. Nehemiah prayed for _____.
2. Moses was told to pray _____ on the people.
3. Most of the Psalms are _____ or prayer _____.
4. Solomon prayed for _____ to lead the people of God.
5. Daniel prayed for _____.

Answers on page 136.

New Testament Prayers of Paul

The prayers of Paul are excellent guides in praying for others and for ourselves. He usually begins each letter by saying, "For God is my witness, whom I serve with my spirit in the gospel of his Son, that without ceasing I make mention of you always in my prayers" (Romans 1:9).

Paul wrote to Timothy: "I exhort therefore, that, first of all, supplications, prayers, intercessions, and giving of thanks, be made for all men. . . . that men pray every where, lifting up holy hands, without wrath and doubting" (1 Timothy 2:1, 8).

In Romans Paul prayed, "Now the God of hope *fill you with*

all joy and peace in believing, that ye may abound in hope, through the power of the Holy Ghost" (15:13).

He requested that the Romans pray for him, "That I may be delivered from them that do not believe in Judaea; and that my service which I have for Jerusalem may be accepted of all the saints; That I may come unto you with joy by the will of God, and may with you be refreshed" (15:31, 32).

He asked the Ephesians to pray "that utterance may be given unto me, that *I may open my mouth boldly, to make known the mystery of the gospel*" (6:19).

To the Ephesians Paul wrote, "[I] cease not to give thanks for you, making mention of you in my prayers; That the God of our Lord Jesus Christ, the Father of glory, may give unto you the spirit of wisdom and revelation in the knowledge of him. The eyes of your understanding being enlightened; *that ye may know what* is *the hope of his calling,* and what the *riches of the glory of his inheritance* in the saints, And what is the exceeding *greatness of his power to* us-ward who believe, according to the working of his mighty power" (1:16-19).

To the Colossians he wrote, "We . . . do not cease to pray for you, and to desire that ye *might be filled with the knowledge of his will* in wisdom and spiritual understanding; That ye might walk worthy of the Lord unto all pleasing, being fruitful in every good work, and increasing in the knowledge of God; Strengthened with all might according to his glorious power, unto all patience and longsuffering with joyfulness" (1:9-11).

Throughout this book the King James Version of the Bible has been used. But here I would like to repeat Paul's prayers in Ephesians and Colossians from the *New International Version.* You may compare them.

"I keep asking that the God of our Lord Jesus Christ, the glorious Father, may give you the Spirit of wisdom and revelation, so that you may know him better. I pray also that the eyes of your heart may be enlightened in order that you may know the hope to which he has called you, the riches of his glorious inheritance in the saints, and his incomparably great power for us who believe" (Ephesians 1:17-19).

"We have not stopped praying for you and asking God to fill you with the knowledge of his will through all spiritual wisdom and understanding. And we pray this in order that you may live a life worthy of the Lord and may please him in every way: bearing fruit in every good work, growing in the knowledge of God, being strengthened with all power according to his glorious might so that you may have great endurance and patience" (Colossians 1:9-11).

And now a final prayer from Paul from the *NIV*: "For this reason I kneel before the Father, from whom his whole family in heaven and on earth derives its name. *I pray that out of his glorious riches he may strengthen you with power through his Spirit in your inner being, so that Christ may dwell in your hearts through faith. And I pray that you, being rooted and established in love, may have power, together with all the saints, to grasp how wide and long and high and deep is the love of Christ, and to know this love that surpasses knowledge—that you may be filled to the measure of all the fullness of God*" (Ephesians 3:14-19).

What a powerful prayer is given in those six verses. If we would pray that for ourselves and others we would surely be enriched in our life.

A Special Word

Someone said that if you have time you can pray long, beautiful, deep prayers; but there are times when all you can do is run and fall on your knees and, as you slide across the floor, cry out, "O God, I need You. Have mercy on me."

It is the burden of your heart, sincerity, integrity, clean hands, a pure heart, and honest searching that God requires.

Whether you are praying for others, for guidance, salvation, healing, social concerns, evangelism, wisdom, understanding, nations, leaders—whatever—*focus on God*. Don't focus on your needs or your problems; focus on the Lord of Glory who has the answer for every need.

Paul prayed for the Thessalonians: *"May he strengthen your hearts so that you will be blameless and holy in the presence of our God and Father when our Lord Jesus comes with all his holy ones"* (1 Thessalonians 3:13, *NIV*).

> ## UNDERSTANDING WHAT YOU READ
>
> In this section we have looked at some of Paul's prayers and the things he prayed for.
>
> 1. Paul was a great believer of prayer and he _____ it constantly.
> 2. Paul also frequently requested prayer for _____.
> 3. The other version of the Bible quoted in this chapter is the _____.
> 4. Paul prayed that _____ might dwell in their hearts and that they might be rooted and established in _____ (Ephesians 3).
> 5. Paul prayed basically for the development of the _____ believers.
>
> *Answers on page 137.*

Our most common type of prayer is conversational prayer, just talking to God out of our love, our heart, our needs, and our burdens.

At other times we intercede for the needs of friends, our pastor, our church, our government officials. And we may use the biblical prayers to bless and to pray for protection and growth.

Praying Hymns

Let us not overlook the rich treasures of prayers in our hymns and spiritual songs. We should sing love songs to the Lord. We should sing our praises and thanksgiving, and even our petitions. From memory or even with the aid of your hymnal, use hymns in your devotions.

From my memory I will list several titles to illustrate: "Come Holy Spirit, I Need Thee," "Just As I Am," "To Be Like Jesus," "I Will Serve Thee Because I Love Thee," "How Great Thou Art," "My Jesus, I Love Thee," "Do Not Pass Me By," "Higher Ground," "Make Me a Blessing,"

"Nearer My God to Thee," "O I Want to See Him," "We Shall Behold Him."

Make these into prayers as you sing them or quote them. Meditate on the meaning. This is scriptural: "Be filled with the Spirit; Speaking to yourselves in psalms and hymns and spiritual songs, singing and making melody in your heart to the Lord" (Ephesians 5:18, 19). "Sing unto God, ye kingdoms of the earth; O sing praises unto the Lord" (Psalm 68:32). "Come before his presence with singing" (Psalm 100:2).

In 2 Chronicles 20 a great battle was won with prayer and singing of praises. The singers went before the army "and when they began to sing and to praise" (v. 22) their enemies destroyed each other.

UNDERSTANDING WHAT YOU READ

In this section we have considered singing as part of our praying.

1. We are to sing and make melody in our heart to _____.
2. When the children of Israel began to sing and to praise in 2 Chronicles 20, their enemies were destroyed by _____.
3. We are instructed to make _____ in our heart to the Lord.

Answers on page 137.

FOR FURTHER STUDY

Book of Nehemiah
Church Hymnal

SELF-CHECK TEST

After you have read chapter eight, complete the brief self-check test. Check your answers on page 139. Then go on to chapter nine.

List

1. Name at least five hymns or choruses that *you know* and that you feel would be beneficial to sing as prayers or praises to the Lord.

    a. _____
    b. _____
    c. _____
    d. _____
    e. _____

2. List at least five things Jesus taught us to pray for in the Lord's Prayer.

    a. _____
    b. _____
    c. _____
    d. _____
    e. _____

Circle T if True and F if False

T F 3. The Holy Spirit helps us when we pray by praying for us according to God's will.

T F 4. "The Lord bless thee, and keep thee, make his face to shine upon thee, be gracious unto thee, and give thee peace" is a blessing that God asked David to use in blessing the people.

T F   5. We are to pray to God for all things—every concern of our life.
T F   6. Paul not only prayed for others, he frequently requested prayer for himself.
T F   7. Most of the Psalms can be prayed.
T F   8. Nehemiah requested that he be given permission to go back to Israel to rebuild the wall of Jericho.
T F   9. Blessings are promised to all who pray for the peace of Jerusalem.
T F 10. Solomon requested that the Lord make him the richest of all kings.

CHAPTER IX

How to Spend a Day in Prayer

A DAY IN PRAYER

In this chapter we want to plan how to spend a day apart in prayer. We can pack a lunch or we can plan to make it a day of prayer and fasting. This is to be a day set aside to meet with God. The primary objective is fellowship with God. It is a time of growing in our devotion to Him, a time of further developing our personal relationship with Him. It is a time of meditation and worship. These are the same goals as our daily "quiet time," whatever the length of time.

Place

First we want to decide on a place where we can be alone, away from distractions. This may be in a wooded area, your backyard, a nearby park, a motel room. Find the place best suited to your needs and personality, best suited to your location, your sense of freedom, privacy, and safety—a place where you can be totally free to focus on God.

Helps

Some useful items will be your Bible—or two or three Bibles of different versions—pencil, notebook, hymnbook, and colored markers. You may want to include a devotional book. I like to have available a concordance for locating scriptures on the same topic.

Plan

Divide the day into parts. One idea is suggested in the simple acrostic ACTS—Adoration, Confession, Thanksgiving, and Supplication.

Adoration

In the period of adoration we concentrate on the greatness and goodness of God. We come into His presence and seek to know Him. We wait before Him and realize His presence. We may sing to Him, adore Him, tell Him we love Him, read such biblical passages as Isaiah 6, Psalm 5, Psalm 23, Revelation 21:1-7. We meditate on His character, His attributes, His power, and yet His tenderness; His justice and yet His mercy; His judgment and yet His pardon.

Just to sit in His presence changes us. When we sit in the rays of the sun we bring part of the glow inside on our body. After Moses talked with God his face glowed (Exodus 34:29, 35). As we sit in the presence of the Son of God, we also will bear His radiance in our countenance and in our spirit.

Do you know the little song entitled, "A Love Song to Jesus" or "In Moments Like These"? This is a good example of an appropriate response to His presence.

> In moments like these
> I sing out a song,
> I sing out a love song to Jesus;
> In moments like these
> I lift up my hands,
> I lift up my hands to the Lord.
>
> Singing, I love You, Lord;
> Singing, I love You, Lord,
> Singing, I love You, Lord,
>   I love You.
>
> Singing, I praise Your name
> Singing, I praise Your name
> Singing, I praise You, Lord
>   I praise You.

> Singing, Hallelujah
> Singing, Hallelujah
> Singing, Hallelujah
> Hallelujah.
>
> —*David Graham*

Confession

In confession we spend time in waiting before the Lord for cleansing and for reaffirmation of our position in Him. We ask God to search our heart. We confess weakness, failures, commission of wrongs, and omission of rights. In Psalm 51 David confesses his sin and prays: "Wash me, renew, restore, uphold me, have mercy on me, open my eyes, purge me."

Then we should confess the positive confession that we are His, He is ours, and we believe His promises. We should renew our commitment to Him: "I love You. You have washed me and cleansed me and forgiven me. My name is written in Your Book of Life. I have been set free from the bondage of Satan. I have been delivered from darkness to light. I am Yours now and for eternity."

"Your word declares, and I believe your word, that 'If we confess our sins, he is faithful and just to forgive us our sins, and to cleanse us from all unrighteousness' (1 John 1:9). 'The blood of Jesus Christ his Son cleanseth us from all sin'" (1 John 1:7).

If we remember that there is something we need to make right, we must make a note and a commitment to do so as soon as possible. Our confession and our cleansing must involve a right relationship with God and a right relationship with others.

A legend is told of the famous artist Leonardo da Vinci. It says that for the face of Judas he painted the face of one of his worst enemies. Later he was having difficulty in painting the face of Christ. He became troubled and could not sleep. Rushing one morning to his studio, he erased the face of his enemy from the figure of Judas. Then he was able to see clearly the face of Christ which he wished to paint.

The Bible declares that "Your iniquities have separated between you and your God, and your sins have hid his face from you, that he will not hear" (Isaiah 59:2). But the Bible also says that you will find him if you look for him with all your heart and with all your soul (Deuteronomy 4:29).

> ## UNDERSTANDING WHAT YOU READ
>
> In this section we have started looking at how to plan for a day of prayer.
> 1. The simple acrostic that we are considering now is _____.
> 2. The first two initials stand for _____ and _____.
> 3. Four items that are most useful to include in a day of prayer are _____, _____, _____, _____.
> 4. A good private place for you to spend a day in prayer would be _____.
>
> *Answers on page 137.*

Thanksgiving

The proper way to come before the Lord, the King of the universe, is with thanksgiving and praise (Psalm 100:4). In Psalm 22:3 we are reminded that God inhabits or dwells in the praises of His people. So if we want His immediate presence, let us praise Him.

Paul Billheimer in *Destined for the Throne* reminds us, "Satan is paralyzed, bound, and banished." We need to thank Jesus constantly for this great truth which He made to be a reality for us. Such expressions as, "Thank You, praise You, glory, hallelujah, worthy art Thou, honor, majesty, glory be unto Thee" bring victory, joy, and deliverance to us.

It is good to count our blessings. It is good to remember from where the Lord has brought us. Look at Solomon's prayer in 1 Kings 8:15-28:

> And he said, Blessed be the Lord God of Israel, which spake with his mouth unto David my father, and hath with his

hand fulfilled it, saying, Since the day that I brought forth my people Israel out of Egypt, I chose no city out of all the tribes of Israel to build an house, that my name might be therein; but I chose David to be over my people Israel. And it was in the heart of David my father to build an house for the name of the Lord God of Israel. . . . And the Lord hath performed his word that he spake, and I am risen up in the room of David my father, and sit on the throne of Israel, as the Lord promised, and have built an house for the name of the Lord God of Israel. . . . And Solomon stood before the altar of the Lord in the presence of all the congregation of Israel, and spread forth his hands toward heaven: And he said, *Lord God of Israel, there is no God like thee, in heaven above, or on earth beneath, who keepest covenant and mercy with thy servants* that walk before thee with all their heart: Who hast kept with thy servant David my father that thou promisedst him. . . . Have thou respect unto the prayer of thy servant, and to his supplication, O Lord my God, to hearken unto the cry and to the prayer, which thy servant prayeth before thee to day.

John the Revelator lets us look on a scene in heaven where the angels and the elders stood around the throne and worshiped God, saying,

Amen: Blessing, and glory, and wisdom, and thanksgiving, and honour, and power, and might, be unto our God for ever and ever. Amen (Revelation 7:12).

Jesus himself also practiced prayer with thanksgiving: At the resurrection of Lazarus, "Jesus lifted up his eyes, and said, Father, *I thank thee* that thou hast heard me" (John 11:41). And in the feeding of the four thousand in Mark 8:6, "He took the seven loaves, and *gave thanks*, and brake, and gave to his disciples to set before them."

Paul instructs the Ephesians to *give thanks always for all things* unto God (Ephesians 5:20). And to the Thessalonians he writes: "Pray without ceasing. *In every thing give thanks:* for this is the will of God in Christ Jesus concerning you" (1 Thessalonians 5:17, 18).

Supplication

Now we have come to the asking part of our prayer. And it is all right to ask—both for others and for ourselves.

The act of asking for others we call *intercession*. The work of Christ is that of an intercessor. The work of the Holy Spirit includes intercession for us according to the will of God

(Romans 8:26, 27). Thus, the work of the church—the people, the saints—should be that of intercessors.

To intercede is to meditate, to bring together lost persons and a saving God, sick people and a healing God, hurting people and a comforting God.

If Christ and the Holy Spirit live in us, we will pray.

Praying the Scriptures

A good way to intercede for others and to petition for ourselves is to pray the Scriptures. When we pray the Scriptures we know that we are praying in God's will.

For example, we can pray with confidence for the salvation of others, knowing that we are praying the will of God since His Word tells us that the Lord is "not willing that any should perish, but that all should come to repentance" (2 Peter 3:9).

A missionary's wife experienced a period of deep depression. One thing her husband did to help her was to pray Romans 15:13 for her: "Now the God of hope fill you with all joy and peace in believing, that ye may abound in hope, through the power of the Holy Ghost."

Jeremiah says that God is active, watching over His word to carry it out, "I will hasten my word to perform it" (1:12). Isaiah says that His Word will not return void, but will accomplish that which He pleases and purposes (55:11). God sent His Word about healing to heal, and His Word about salvation to save.

Also praying the Word increases our faith. "Faith cometh by hearing, and hearing by the word of God" (Romans 10:17).

Harrison House has published a small book, *Praying God's Word*, by Ed Dufresne Ministries. Prayers composed of passages of Scripture are suggested for congregations, ministers, ministries, families, wives, children, husbands, unsaved, and others.

Here is one example based on the King James and the *Amplified Bible* praying for the body of Christ, the Church:

> Father, in the name of Jesus, I bring before You the body of believers of _____ and all over the world. I confess with my mouth, through faith in Your Word, that we let no foul or polluting language, nor evil word, nor unwhole-

some or worthless talk, (ever) come out of our mouth; but only such speech as is good and beneficial to the spiritual progress of others, as is fitting to the need and the occasion, that it may be a blessing and give grace to those who hear it. I say that we let all bitterness and indignation and wrath (passion, rage, bad temper) and resentment (anger, animosity, and quarreling, brawling, clamor, contention) and slander (evil speaking, abrasive or blasphemous language) be banished from us, with all malice (spite, ill will, or baseness of any kind).

And we have become useful and helpful and tenderhearted (compassionate, understanding, loving hearted) and kind to one another, forgiving one another (readily and freely) as You, in Christ, forgave us. Thank You, Father, that we walk in love, esteeming and delighting in one another as Christ loved us and gave Himself up for us, a slain offering and sacrifice to You.

I thank You that You watch over Your Word to perform it. I believe that I have received this, according to Mark 11:23, 24, in Jesus' Name. Amen.

(Ephesians 4:29, 31, 32; 5:1, 2 [*Amplified*]; Colossians 4:2; James 4:16; 1 Corinthians 1:30).

This is just an example as to how you may use the Scriptures as goals for growth. Ask your prayer partner, your friends, "Is there any scripture, any promise of God, that you would like me to pray for you?" Pray the promises of God for one another and with one another.

I would like my friends to pray Paul's Ephesian prayer for me:

That according to the riches of his [God's] glory, to be strengthened with might by his Spirit, in the inner man; That Christ may dwell in your [my] hearts by faith; that ye [I], being rooted and grounded in love, May be able to comprehend with all saints what is the breadth, and length, and depth, and height; And to know the love of Christ, which passeth knowledge, that ye [I] might be filled with all the fulness of God (Ephesians 3:16-18).

From Paul also we can pray such good things as, "That ye walk worthy of the vocation wherewith ye are called. . . . That ye put off . . . the former conversation [of] the old man . . . [and] be renewed in the spirit of your mind" (Ephesians 4:1, 22, 23). Also we should pray "that utterance may be given unto me, that I may open my mouth boldly, to make known the mystery of the gospel, For which I am an ambassador" (6:19, 20).

> ## UNDERSTANDING WHAT YOU READ
> In this section we have considered two more facets of a plan for spending a day in prayer.
> 1. The third and fourth letters of the acrostic ACTS stand for _____ and _____.
> 2. Solomon stood before the altar of the Lord and _____ his hands toward heaven and _____.
> 3. Instead of worrying, we are to tell God what we need and _____ Him.
> 4. The prayer of talking with God for others is called _____.
>
> *Answers on page 137.*

Keep a Notebook

It is a good to have a notebook at our place of prayer. It serves many purposes. In it we can keep a prayer list and we can record answers to prayers.

If we write down insights from the Word we will remember them better. As we listen to what God is saying to us we can make notes. Perhaps He is reminding us of someone we should call, visit, or write.

Sometimes the words of a hymn, which we have not sung in years, will come fresh again to our memory. Or it may be a poem.

Write down praises and thanks to God. A record of prayers, answers, and thankfulness will build your faith and deepen your devotion.

Prayer for Yourself

This was included somewhat in our discussion of praying the Scriptures. However, a little more needs to be said.

God wants you to share with Him all the secrets of your heart. He knows them, but He will not intrude. You must invite Him to share these with you. Bring to Him decisions that you need to make. He promises that if you will acknowledge Him in all your ways, He will direct your paths (Proverbs 3:6).

Ask the Lord for understanding. Meditate on His Word. When you read the Bible ask: What does it say? What does it mean? How does that affect me? Is there anything I should do about it?

Someone has suggested an acrostic for Bible reading and meditation using the vowels AEIOU. They stand for:

Ask—Who, What, When, Where, Why, How—What does the passage say?

Emphasize—Put emphasis on key words. Study the words.

Interpret—Put it in your own words. Paraphrase.

Other Passages—Compare related scriptures.

Use—What should you do about it? What action or obedience is needed?

Jesus taught us in the Lord's Prayer to ask for daily bread, forgiveness of sin, not to be led into temptation, deliverance from evil, His will to be done, His kingdom to come. Meditate on the prayers of Jesus recorded in the New Testament.

We should pray that we may do the work that He has given us to do and not be overly occupied by the cares and problems of life. Jesus said, "My meat [food] is to do the will of him who sent me and to finish his work" (John 4:34).

We should check the use of our time, our resources, our talents, our finances, and our associations that they are being used to further His kingdom. What are we doing to finish His work?

Some people walk and pray. Some pace the floor. Some sit at a table. Others like to be on the floor, on their knees. Try variety. Pray in any and all positions.

Bring problems. If you reach conclusions or specific direction, make notes. If something pops into your mind that needs to be done, jot it down.

At the end of the day, summarize what God has spoken to you about, what more you have learned about Him, and what He wants you to be and to do.

> ## UNDERSTANDING WHAT YOU READ
> In this section we looked at keeping a notebook, praying for yourself, and we briefly talked about meditation.
> 1. List at least four ways you can use the notebook during prayer time: _____, _____, _____, _____.
> 2. What do the letters AEIOU represent as a meditation acrostic? _____, _____, _____, _____, _____.
> 3. As you summarize what you have learned; make special note of what God wants you to _____ and to _____.
> *Answers on page 137.*

Note: Enlarged Plan

For a plan broken into 12 parts, read *The Hour That Changes the World* by Dick Eastman. He begins and ends with praise. The segments are as follows and there is a chapter setting forth each segment:

1. Praise—The Act of Divine Adoration (Psalm 63:3) Recognizing God's Nature

2. Waiting—The Act of Soul Surrender (Psalm 46:10) Silent Soul Surrender

3. Confession—The Act of Declared Admission (Psalm 139:23)   Simple Cleansing Time

4. Scripture Praying—The Act of Faith Appropriation (Jeremiah 23:29)   Word-Enriched Prayer

5. Watching—The Act of Mental Awareness (Colossians 4:2)   Develop Holy Alertness

6. Intercession—The Act of Earnest Appeal (1 Timothy 2:1, 2)   Remember the World

7. Petition—The Act of Personal Supplication (Matthew 7:7)   Share Personal Needs

8. Thanksgiving—The Act of Expressed Appreciation (1 Thessalonians 5:18)   Confess My Blessings
9. Singing—The Act of Melodic Worship (Psalm 100:2) Worship in Song
10. Meditation—The Act of Spiritual Evaluation (James 1:8) Ponder Spiritual Themes
11. Listening—The Act of Mental Absorption (Ecclesiastes 5:2)   Receive Spiritual Instruction
12. Praise—The Act of Divine Magnification (Psalm 52:9) Recognizing God's Nature

I believe we have included all of these in the shorter form, but you will find Eastman's book helpful in planning extended periods of prayer.

Examples

One pastor spends a day a month at a nearby retreat center trying to clear his mind of problems and refocus on the broad goals of ministry.

Another spends a day a week at the local library in a time of quietness before God.

In Korea and Taiwan, Christians take a day or two off and go to "Prayer Mountain," a place apart, for time with God.

Herbert and I visited Dr. Cho's church in Seoul, Korea. It is the largest Pentecostal church in the world. "We teach the people to pray until they touch God," we were told. Buses leave daily for "Prayer Mountain" where thousands pray daily.

Terry Muck, in the spring volume of *Leadership* 1985, talks about the approach developed by Harold Ockenga, pastor of Park Street Church in Boston who at the same time served as president of Fuller Theological Seminary:

> I've always been very busy, but I feel there is a secret. My secret was administration by prayer. For forty-one years I have kept everything on a detailed prayer list:
>
> - I kept problems on there—when I went over it daily I was reminded by the Lord if I hadn't done anything about them. . . .
> - I kept a list of people I disagreed with on my prayer list so I could pray for them, asking the Lord to change the situation between us. . . .

- Of course, I also kept special requests on my list.

When any of these prayers were answered, I would just write *Answered* across the notation. . . .

Keeping this list kept me alert to my responsibilities, the chief one being my need to bring everything to God in prayer (Vol. 6, #2, p. 47).

FASTING

Often those who spend a day in prayer, combine it with fasting. R. A. Torrey in his book, *How to Pray*, says: "If we would pray with power, we should pray with fasting. This of course does not mean that we should fast every time we pray; but there are times in emergency or special crisis . . . when men of downright earnestness will withdraw themselves even from the gratification of the natural appetites that . . . they may give themselves up wholly to prayer."

Jesus fasted (Matthew 4:2). The early church fasted and prayed (Acts 10:30; 13:2). Using your concordance, study fasting in the Old and New Testaments.

Fasting means to do without, to practice self-denial. This includes not only food but also other things that hinder our communion with God.

Primarily, however, fasting means "not to eat." In the Bible fasting took three main forms: The first, the normal fast, meant abstaining from all food, solid or liquid, but not from water.

The second is the absolute fast, as in Acts 9:9, when we neither eat nor drink. Normally this is not for more than three days. The body can go long periods without food and be physically benefited, but it can go only for a short time without water.

The third, the partial fast, as in Daniel 10:3, restricts the diet rather than abstaining. It may also consist of omitting certain meals each day for a time. It is of special value when circumstances prevent a normal fast.

Fasting may be public or private, regular or occasional, voluntary or involuntary.

In *God's Chosen Fast*, Arthur Wallis says, "Whenever in Scripture we read of a public emergency being met by a national call to fast, we find without exception that God responded in deliverance."

It is a good thing to check up on our prayer life from time to time. Is it continuing to be an effective force in my life? Do I need to change some facet of it? Have I gotten into a rut or a habit? Do I need to meditate more, spend more time listening? Do I need to sing more to the Lord, take notes, pray aloud, walk and pray? Do I need to add variety? Am I putting into practice the lessons of my prayer life?

UNDERSTANDING WHAT YOU READ

In this section we observed some who are putting into practice praying for a day.

1. The "prayer mountain" idea is well developed in _____.
2. Pastor Ockenga said his secret was administration by _____.
3. A facet of prayer that produces great results and needs further study and practice is that of _____ with our prayer.
4. Try to name the 12 segments of Eastman's hour of prayer: _____, _____, _____, _____, _____, _____, _____, _____, _____, _____, _____, _____.

Answers on page 137.

FOR FURTHER STUDY

Wallis, Arthur. *God's Chosen Fast.* London: Victory Press, 1968.
Billheimer, Paul E. *Destined for the Throne.* Minneapolis: Bethany, 1975.
Eastman, Dick. *The Hour That Changes the World.* Grand Rapids: Baker, 1978.
Duewel, Wesley L., *Touch the World Through Prayer.* Grand Rapids, Michigan, Francis Asbury Press, 1986.

SELF-CHECK TEST

After you have read chapter nine and looked up the verses in the Bible, you should take this brief test. Answer the questions without referring back to the text. Look up the answers on page 139. If you had three or four wrong answers, you should read the lesson again, retake the test, and then proceed to chapter ten.

MULTIPLE CHOICE

Choose the answer that best completes the following statements and circle it in pencil or use another sheet to record your answers.

1. The four words that the acrostic ACTS stands for in the prayer plan are . . .
   a. ask, confess, think, sing
   b. adoration, confession, thanksgiving, singing
   c. asking, confessing, thinking, supplication
   d. adoration, confession, thanksgiving, supplication

2. Something to have with you for your day of prayer should be . . .
   a. Bible
   b. notebook
   c. songbook
   d. all of the above

3. Your day of prayer should be spent . . .
   a. outdoors
   b. in your room
   c. at the library
   d. the quiet place best for you

4. The acrostic suggested as a guide in meditation was . . .
   a. EIEIO
   b. AEIOU
   c. UNION
   d. ITATE

5. In confession we spend time . . .
   a. for cleansing
   b. for forgiveness
   c. for declaring our place in Christ
   d. all of the above

6. The legend about the famous painter Leonardo da Vinci states that he could not see a clear picture for painting the face of Christ until . . .

a. he had all the others painted
b. he prayed for a revelation of the face
c. he found a saint to copy
d. he removed the face of his enemy from the figure of Judas

7. The Bible declares that our sins separate us from God and . . .
    a. cause us to have to do penance
    b. hide His face from us
    c. require us to wash in "holy water"
    d. cannot be forgiven

8. The Bible says that God's presence is with people when they . . .
    a. study
    b. work
    c. praise
    d. sacrifice

9. Paul tells us that prayer should always be offered with
    a. thanksgiving
    b. alms
    c. repentance
    d. weeping

10. Intercession is the work of
    a. Jesus Christ
    b. Holy Spirit
    c. Church
    d. all of the above

CHAPTER X

Testimonies of Results of Prayer

RESULTS BEYOND MEASURE

Prayer has many rewards. The results are innumerable. We will look at some of them.

Prayer brings us into the presence of God and makes effective His graces in our life. Through prayer our sins are forgiven, we are born again into God's family, and we enter into a walk in the Spirit that leads us to holiness and wholeness. Beholding Him we are more and more transformed into the image of Christ (2 Corinthians 3:18).

As we open our heart to the Holy Spirit, self is laid aside. His will supersedes our will. His concerns become our concerns. He lives in us and works through us. We are partners with God in His work of redeeming the world.

To illustrate the answers granted to prayer for the extension of the Redeemer's kingdom on earth, it would be necessary to outline the history of the whole church, says D. M. M'Intyre in *The Hidden Life of Prayer*.

For example, M'Intyre points out, "By prayer a handful of 'unlearned and ignorant men,' hard-handed from the oar and the rudder, the mattock and the pruning-hook, 'turned the world upside down,' and spread the name of Christ beyond the limits of the Roman power.

"By prayer the tent-maker of Tarsus won the dissolute Corinthians to purity and faith, laid the enduring foundations of Western Christianity, and raised the name of Jesus high in the very palace of Nero."

The history of the church moves on from age to age and from continent to continent.

M'Intyre shares the account of Robert Roberts whose sermon was the apparent cause of a great awakening in Wales. "Tell me, Roberts, where did you get that wonderful sermon?" a friend asked.

"Come here," said Roberts as he led his friend to a small parlor. "It was here I found that sermon you speak of—on the floor here, all night long, turning backward and forward, with my face sometimes on the earth."

Think of the results of the many kinds of things prayed for in the Bible: Isaac prayed about Rebekah's failure to bear a child. David prayed for counsel in battle. Solomon prayed for wisdom to guide God's people. Elijah prayed for rain. Daniel prayed to interpret dreams. Nehemiah prayed to be released from exile to go rebuild the wall of Jerusalem. Blind men prayed for sight. Lepers prayed to be clean. Paul prayed for survival in shipwreck. The Christians prayed for Peter's release from prison. Jesus prayed for His followers to be kept faithful in trying times and to be filled with the Holy Spirit.

F. J. Huegel says in *Successful Praying* that in prayer we "enter into the holiest by the blood of Jesus" (Hebrews 10:19). In prayer we take a stand "against the enemy and in the Name of Jesus and on the basis of the victory won at Calvary" we claim release from the powers of darkness. On our knees we may "thrust forth missionaries to the farthermost reaches of a sin-stricken humanity's heathenism."

FRASER

In *Behind the Ranges*, Mrs. Howard Taylor recounts the experience of missionary J. O. Fraser's breakthrough in villages on the China-Burma border. Fraser said it was so hard that he was utterly discouraged and about to give up when a tract fell into his hands focusing his attention upon the fact of his Redeemer's victory over the powers of darkness through His death and resurrection. The tract pointed out that this victory had to be appropriated and released in the form of a command of faith.

Fraser decided to try it. He went out to a desert place hurling the command of faith into the enemy's ranks. He praised God at the top of his lungs. In his Savior's holy name he commanded the enemy and his hosts to flee.

Fraser said it was the turning point of his ministry against paganism. The tide turned and a mighty revival swept through the villages.

David Lemons in *Bread Upon Waters* in reviewing the life and ministry of R. P. Johnson shares:

> Have you ever heard a prophet pray? R. P. Johnson would begin his prayer with "Our Father, who art in heaven," and by the time he would say "hallowed be thy name," the veil that separates the here and the hereafter would part sufficiently for all of us to slip into the "holy place" around the mercy seat.
>
> His prayer would progress in thanksgiving for graces and mercies, past and present. He would intercede for all in authority. Because of his abiding concern and love for the Church of God, he would call the names of the leaders, telling God something of the responsibilities of each one.
>
> The prayer would take on an aura of praise, with eloquence, experienced only by prophetic inspiration. Then what happened can only be understood by spiritual concept. It seemed that the angels above the mercy seat would wave their wings so that zephyrs of heaven would fan the already fervent prayer into a glow of glory. And those long arms and great hands that had often blessed many people seemed to reach out into infinity.
>
> With this grasp on God and this reach toward man, he would call the names of needy, sorrowing, sick, and suffering ones at his altar of prayer.
>
> Oblivious to time and distance, he invoked divine blessings upon his loving wife, his faithful pastor, each member of his family, his children, and each member of their families. And prior to the conclusion of this phase of his prayer he would say, "And oh, heavenly Father, what we ask for these, we would ask for all Your children everywhere. . . ."
>
> The preaching of R. P. Johnson was often accented with shouts of praise and rejoicing, sometimes with dancing in the Spirit, sometimes with weeping, and always with evidence of seasoning with prayer.

Read the book *Azusa Street*, a reprint of Bartleman's 1925 history of how Pentecost came to Los Angeles. It is a story of prayer and fasting, of all day and all night intercession. It was "the fellowship of His suffering," of "travail" of soul, with "groanings that could not be uttered." Soon the Pentecostal outpouring spread around the world.

> ## UNDERSTANDING WHAT YOU READ
> In this section we have given a brief overview of some of the results of prayers of many kinds for a variety of needs.
> 1. In prayer we are more and more transformed into the image of _____.
> 2. M'Intyre said if we were to illustrate the answers granted to prayer for the extension of God's kingdom, we would have to outline the _____.
> 3. Prayer leads us into the life of holiness and _____.
> 4. Roberts got that revival awakening sermon _____
>
> *Answers on page 137.*

More things are wrought by prayer
Than this world dreams of.
Wherefore, let thy voice
Rise like a fountain for me night and day.
For what are men better than sheep and goats
That nourish a blind life within the brain,
If, knowing God, they lift not hands of prayer
Both for themselves and those
Who call them friend?
For so the whole round earth is every way
Bound by gold chains about the feet of God.
—Alfred Lord Tennyson

Villancas of Peru

One of the most beautiful accounts of prayer that brings together a pray-er with the answer and a pray-er with a need is one recounted by T. R. Morse of the Church of God World Missions Department. It is like the account of Paul and Ananias (Acts 9) or Cornelius and Peter (Acts 10).

In 1961 when Morse was assistant superintendent of Latin America, Sister Villanca of Peru shared this testimony with him which the department prepared in tract form:

> Upon graduation from Bible school my husband was appointed to a small church in the foothills of the Andes Mountains. The church did not support us sufficiently, since we had two

children, so Juan took a job on the construction of the International Highway, at an amount equivalent to fifty cents U.S. money a day.

Several weeks ago, after we had our breakfast, I had packed a lunch for Juan and he had gone to work, I felt a burden of prayer and went behind the house, leaving the children asleep, and knelt to pray.

The Lord spoke to me and said that He wanted my husband and me to go to an Indian village which was 300 kilometers—approximately 180 miles—across two snow-capped mountains to take the gospel to a certain tribe of people.

I talked to the Lord and told Him that I was not the head of the family nor the preacher; that He would have to speak to my husband, as I could not give the answer.

Then the Lord seemed to ask me if I would be willing to go with my husband on the missionary journey.

I told the Lord I was willing to go anywhere and do anything for Him.

After prayer I busied myself with my home and family, until my husband returned for the evening meal. I asked him to hurry and offer thanks for the meal as I had something very important to talk to him about.

He asked the blessing and then stated that he had something to tell me.

We argued back and forth a little, as I thought mine was more important and I felt I needed to talk to him first about what the Lord had impressed upon me as I prayed.

I had assumed that he wanted to tell me something that some of the men had talked about on the job that day, or something about his work.

However, being an obedient wife, I listened while he spoke. And to my surprise, Juan began to tell me how at lunchtime, though he had always eaten lunch with the men, today he felt impressed to be alone as he felt a spirit of prayer.

He said the Lord spoke to him and asked him if he would go to that same Indian village 300 kilometers away to take the gospel message. Juan asked me if I would be willing to go.

In tears, I told him this was exactly the same thing I had wanted to talk to him about, as the Lord had impressed me earlier in the morning.

My husband gave two weeks' notice to leave his work on the highway, which also gave us time to select some blankets and a few clay pots and to get our beans and rice ready for the journey.

Of course there were no airlines going to this place. . . . There were no buses because there were no highways for them. There was no transportation at all, since we did not have a donkey.

Therefore, the only thing for us to do was to take the two children, our packs of blankets, cooking utensils, and food, and start walking.

At the end of the first day's walk we were invited into a person's home along the trail.

The next night we spent along the path, wrapped in our blankets.

During the two weeks it took us to make the journey, our food ran out. We slept in the cold snow. The children cried because they were hungry and cold. But the Lord had given us a call and we must carry out His Great Commission to go into all the world and preach the gospel to every creature.

Nothing could stop us from reaching our destination.

As we came near the village where we were to witness, the small children came down the mountainside and met us.

They asked us who we were, where we were from, and what our business was.

We told them to call for the Chief of their tribe.

He met us in the edge of town and we introduced ourselves. We told him that we were from a town near the capital and inquired of him as to the name of the god his tribe was serving.

He said, "We do not know the name of the god that we are serving."

"All Quechua Indians have many gods and each tribe and village chooses several of these gods for their own," we replied. "They offer sacrifices and pray to them. Surely you must know the names of the gods that you are serving."

He replied that they had had gods, but some weeks ago their people took some kind of plague and began to get sick, and many of them were dying. During this great disaster, they prayed to their gods and offered sacrifices of the best of foods, but still the people got sick and very many died.

At this, the Chief gave instruction for the priest of those gods and the medicine men to pull down the wooden gods, to burn them in the fire and to cast the ashes in the river; also, to pull down the stone gods, crush them and cast them in the river.

Then he called the people together and told them that surely there was one God above all the gods. They were asked to start praying to that God, whoever He was and wherever He was, that He would stop the plague and help their people to live.

They all began to fast and pray at which time, to their amazement, no one else died and those who were sick began to get well. No one else took the disease.

At this the people rejoiced, but the Chief said, "We still do not know the name of this God. I am sure there is someone, somewhere who knows His name."

He stated that on a certain morning about four weeks ago, very early in the morning, he called the people to pray that this God would direct someone to come and tell them His name.

This was the exact time that the Lord had spoken to us to come to this village. . . . I could hold it no longer, and cried, "His name is Jesus! We not only know His name but this same God spoke to us on that same morning and told us to come and tell you His name!"

Holding a Bible out to the people, we told them, "This Book contains the history and record of our Lord and Savior, and from it we will read to you and teach you about Him."

After two weeks' time, all who were old enough had been converted and baptized in water, and most of the people had received the baptism of the Holy Ghost. We stayed about two weeks more, teaching and instructing the people . . . in the Word of God. Then we had to bid them goodbye and take the two-week journey back to our little church.

UNDERSTANDING WHAT YOU READ

In this section we are looking at testimonies of answers to prayer that let us share in the real life experiences of others.

1. This is a true account of how the Villancas traveled to another village to share the gospel in the country of _____.
2. The family traveled to the village by way of _____.
3. It took two _____ to walk from the Villancas' homeplace to the other village.
4. The Chief and his people had prayed asking that someone come to tell them _____.

Answers on page 137.

PIONEER PREACHERS

Christmas

Youth Director Ken Hall said he remembered as a child his dad, a pioneer preacher in Alabama, opening new churches in new towns. There was opposition, persecution, financial deprivations.

During one Christmas season they were living in a small trailer. Ken and his brother slept on a small couch that folded down to make a bed for them. The boys heard their parents talking and then praying as they had retired for the night. "O God," prayed Ken's father, "how can I tell my children that there will be no Christmas? How can I explain that we have no food, no toys? I preach a great God who cares for His children. How can I explain no Christmas?"

The next morning a knock was heard on the trailer door. A Roman Catholic lady and another lady stood there: "Pastor, you came to us and prayed for us in the hospital when we were sick three weeks ago, and God healed us. We thought we would just bring Christmas to you." They brought presents, loads of food, and even a Christmas tree.

Bus Fare

Another pioneer preacher shared an experience that lingers in my heart. He said he was walking to his preaching appointment because he didn't have bus fare.

As he was walking along, he was observing nature, meditating about life, and just talking with God as a friend.

"Lord, it seems strange to me," he said, "that wicked people sometimes have so much in this world. They seem to have money to waste, and Your children hardly have money for food. Some people have fine automobiles and use them to go to sinful places, and Your servant doesn't have bus money to go preach."

Just then he looked down by the side of the road and saw a dead sparrow. He stopped. "Lord, the Bible says that You see all the sparrows that fall. Because this is one of Your little birds, I'm going to bury it."

As he picked up the tiny bird, there under its lifeless body he found the bus fare he needed.

God does see the sparrow. God does hear His children. The lessons of His love and care, of His gentle and unique ways of answering us, are far more valuable and unforgettable than just an instant supply.

UNDERSTANDING WHAT YOU READ

In this section you continue to read testimonies of real-life experiences of people who have experienced answers from God in response to their prayers.

1. Ken Hall as a child was impressed with the power of prayer when two ladies brought food and gifts to his house at _____.
2. The man who found the bus fare under the dead bird was a _____ going to _____.
3. The lessons learned in hard times are often much more _____ and _____ than what we learn when everything is easy and we seem to have all we need.
4. Recall experiences in your own life of God's loving ways of answering your prayers.

Answers on page 137.

Dr. R. Lamar Vest has experienced several outstanding answers to prayer related to his life, his ministry, his health, and his family. He has had a very fruitful ministry as a leader of youth around the world. For 22 years he served in youth leadership—as state and then international director of Youth and Christian Education for the Church of God before becoming president of Lee College and then assistant general overseer.

I know this testimony of just one of those experiences will build your faith and encourage you to avail yourself of the power of prayer.

Lost, A Voice

"Reverend, I have good news and bad news," the physician said. "Which do you want first?" I asked for the good news.

"Well," he began in a very slow, contemplative manner, "the good news is that I don't believe the growth on your vocal cord is malignant." That was bad news! No one had ever told me that I had a growth. I knew now, however, why my family physician was so concerned.

We were living in Oklahoma at the time where I was serving as state youth and Christian education director. I had just returned home from an Oklahoma Prayer Conference in which a very disturbing development had occurred. I had lost my voice during the meeting.

Unable to speak above a slight whisper for several days, I naturally grew increasingly concerned. After much encouragement from my wife, I decided to visit our family physician for an examination. I expected it to be no more than a routine visit and for the doctor to tell me that my voice was suffering from overuse and that I only needed a few days of voice rest. However, it did not take me long to discover that the doctor and I were not in agreement as to the diagnosis.

After an intense exploration in the area of my vocal cords, I detected a very concerned look on the face of the physician. He excused himself for a few minutes and then returned to the room where I sat.

"Reverend," he said, "I don't want to alarm you, but I have called Oklahoma City to arrange for you to see a throat specialist. He can see you next week."

With a great deal of painful effort, in tones something under a whisper, I managed to force the inevitable inquiry, "What's wrong, doctor?"

"I'm not sure," he responded, "but I believe it will be best for us to seek an opinion of someone more trained in this area than I. That's why I want you to go to Oklahoma City."

After examining my vocal cords for a second time, the doctor excused himself and was out of the room for some ten to fifteen minutes. Returning, he announced that he had called the specialist again and had moved my appointment up for the next morning. He never asked if the earlier appointment would fit into my schedule, but began immediately giving me directions to the specialist's office.

My wife and I were at the specialist's office early the next morning. I was his first patient. The examination and periods of waiting lasted most of the day.

"What's the bad news?" I asked.

"The bad news is that we are not going to be able surgically to remove the growth at this time," he responded, adding, after a long pause. "I'm not even sure that we can even successfully remove it, at least not so that you will be able to speak publicly again."

I remember assuring him not to worry, that I felt confident God had called me to preach and that He would see to it that I had a voice with which to declare His Word. He said, "Young man, it's evident that you do not understand the seriousness of your problem." He then proceeded to tell me of several cases similar to mine in which the persons were never able to talk again.

After much discussion between the physician and myself,

and for me it was quite an effort to project my words in an understandable manner, he finally asked if he might speak with my wife. Iris was still in the waiting room.

Following me to the waiting room, the doctor introduced himself to Iris and stated, "You certainly are married to a very persistent person!" However, after hearing the doctor's prognostication, Iris was as persistent as I had been.

"Don't worry doctor," she said. "We're sure that everything is going to be all right. But, we do appreciate your concern."

I was asked to return in two weeks, at which time the doctor said I would begin a program he called "occupational rehabilitation," meaning, I guess, some kind of work which did not require the use of my voice. He insisted that I go on total voice rest for two weeks. The last thing he requested was that I go to a newsstand and purchase a current magazine which had an article about a radio disc jockey who had suffered from the same problem I was experiencing. I did, and it wasn't very encouraging. This radio announcer was able to return to using his voice after a period of two years of total voice rest and subsequent surgery. The doctor had suggested that I might also have to be on voice rest for at least two years.

Iris and I returned to the youth parsonage in Chandler, Oklahoma, and she immediately began calling our family and friends asking them to pray for my healing. I went to the bedroom. Kneeling down beside my bed, with my Bible open, I began to pray. Keeping my promise, I didn't pray audibly, but rather I mentally communicated with God in prayer. My Bible was open to Matthew 21:22, not by my own intentions, but, I believe, by the will of God.

Immediately my eyes fell on those words I had read hundreds of times before. But never had they seemed more real, and especially for me, than they did now. "And all things, whatsoever ye shall ask in prayer, believing, ye shall recieve."

"There it is God," I prayed. "This is Your Word. I didn't write it. It didn't come from any man. These are Your words, God, and I believe them and appropriate them right now."

At that moment I experienced what I believe was the gift of faith. I had no doubt God had answered my prayer and that everything was going to be all right. Getting up from my knees I walked back to the family room where Iris was on her knees praying. Tapping her on the shoulder, I handed her a note that read, "Honey, everything is AOK. I'm going to the office to check today's mail."

I never prayed again for God to heal me. I was sure that my prayer had been answered and that it would be redundant for me to pray for healing anymore.

Two weeks later Iris and I were back in the doctor's office in Oklahoma City. She asked if she would be permitted to go with me into the examining room, and was allowed to do so. I was still not talking, being true to my promise not to use my voice for the two-week period. After a courteous exchange of greetings between Iris and the doctor, I was asked to sit down in the dental-like examining chair.

The examination only took a few minutes. The doctor turned off the bright overhead light and began washing his hands in the small lavatory in the corner of the room. Turning around, he exclaimed, "I just don't understand it!"

"What's the problem?" Iris asked.

"The problem is, there is no problem," the doctor responded. "I can't find anything wrong with this man's throat."

I gladly and quickly obliged the doctor's request to test my voice, speaking as clearly as I have ever spoken.

Before leaving his office, I asked the doctor if I should come back for a future examination. "You don't ever have to come back to this office," he said. "You just keep preaching and believing what you have been preaching and believing."

That is what I have been doing since that eventful day in February, 1968.

A Hot Night in New York City

Among the many experiences Herbert and I have had in the ministry over the years—youth camps USA, missions in Haiti, Europe, Israel, college campus life—one of our most difficult and most rewarding assignments was in New York City. We worked there with David Wilkerson in his street ministries to runaways, drug addicts, alcoholics, prostitutes, Black Panthers. I want to share with you a couple of experiences there. One is the experience of just one special night at our coffee house ministry in Manhattan:

It was a hot night. Tempers flared. One could feel the vibrations of riot and rebellion. A group was already gathered on the street in front of our station which we called "God's Living Room."

A group beating on the lids of trash cans yelled, "Give us Bob (a street guy). He held a knife on Spring (a street girl) today and ripped off her carton of chocolate milk. We don't do that to each other. We're gonna take care of him."

A riot was building. Could Bob run for it and make it? No! "We'll get him when he comes out," the yells came.

Finally we decided we would do something we had not done in all our operation there. We decided to call the 911 number and ask for a police escort for Bob to a place of safety in order to prevent a riot and save Bob.

In a short while the police came and walked Bob out to the squad car and took him out of the area.

We tried to continue the regular operation of the coffee house—giving free food, witnessing, listening to young people—but the angry mob lingered. From floors above, someone began dropping plastic bags of water on the heads of the group outside our door. "We'll burn the place down," they yelled.

All the workers began to pray. We were an ecumenical group of Spirit-filled Christians and we were dedicating our lives to witnessing to the street people. "Lord, give us direction," we prayed. Then we made another unusual decision: "We are closing the 'Living Room' except for those who wish to stay and pray. Anyone wishing to pray may stay. Everyone else should move on."

It was a miracle. The mob moved on. We locked the door and those inside sat down and started praying.

I was sitting with my eyes closed and my arms lifted praising God when I heard a sharp knock on the glass front. A policeman beckoned me.

What I saw shocked me. Police cars had come from both directions and had blocked off the street from both ends. Police were out of their cars with clubs in hand.

But there were no street kids. "Where are they?" the leader asked. "We sent them away," I said. "A riot seemed inevitable so we closed up. We're just praying now."

The man who had brought the squad was very angry. He was embarrassed. "Don't you ever ask us to help you again! You baby these bums and then want us to help."

They had come to fight it out with the street people. We learned that just that day a bomb had blown up one of the restrooms at the police station and the police blamed the street kids. When the police had come to pick up Bob and had seen the mob, they had decided to have a confrontation.

God had saved us from a very dangerous, life-threatening possibility. When we could have been battling for our lives we were sitting with arms raised praising Him. His Spirit had intervened.

Just a short time before in our daily prayer and Bible study time with the workers, the Holy Spirit had said: "I send you forth as sheep among wolves. But do not be afraid. For I am your heavenly Father and I will take care of you."

Let me tell you also about Stephen. He represents the kind

STEPHEN

Stephen came in, walking in a fog, out of touch with the world about him, hardly able to stand. Stephen looked young and clean, about twenty-two; his French cuffs now hung loose, unlinked. His face was flushed and his eyes refused to focus. When someone spoke directly to him, he would turn his head like a mannequin to stare directly into the speaker's face and often would respond with an illogical laugh.

Stephen was on a heavy drug trip. He had started it about 36 hours earlier but was still far out of reach. He needed someone to talk with him to help him control the trip and bring his mind back into focus.

I picked up the book, *Masterpieces of Biblical Art*, that our pastor had sent us and began to direct his attention to the pictures and read to him the accompanying scriptures. I began with the picture of Christ knocking at the door. I read the beautiful words from Revelation 3:20: "Behold, I stand at the door and knock: in any man hear my voice, and open the door, I will come in to him and will sup with him and he with me."

"Read that again!" Steve requested. So I read it again and talked of the love of Jesus Christ, our need of Him, and of His power to deliver us.

After a while, I put my hand on Steve's temple and prayed for him. "Pray that again, that felt so good." So I prayed again. Then I asked him to pray with me. And he repeated: "Jesus, I open the door of my heart to You to let You in. Jesus, come in and never leave me. Jesus, save me."

From the Gospel of Luke I read of Jesus' healing the sick, raising the dead, curing lepers, casting out demons. Stephen would say, "Read more." Finally I tried to excuse myself so that I could take my turn serving chocolate, coffee, and cookies. I was the older hostess in the coffee house outreach center. Even though each worker could feel free to deal personally with persons who entered, there was also the responsibility to share with the care of the entire operation and to keep an outlook on the total balance of the program.

But before I got to the kitchen area, Steve caught up with

me, pleading, "Please, let's talk some more." "All right, you talk to me," I replied. "Tell me about yourself and your family." But he would not talk. "Let's talk about what's in *you*. Let's talk about Jesus," he requested.

So I read more Scripture. And as I read he would pray—"Jesus, save me; Jesus, Jesus."

After praying with him again, I told him that I would give him a copy of the New Testament that he could take with him and read. I started to write "To Stephen," but he said, "Stephen is a bad person: write 'To Jesus.'" So I wrote, "To Stephen because of the love of Jesus." Then I read to him the story of Stephen in the Bible and how he had lived and died for Christ. He wanted that read a second time also.

After several hours Stephen walked out into the drizzling cold rain—out in the city—out of our lives.

We give thanks that he encountered the power of prayer, the Word of God, the touch of love, the name of Jesus.

UNDERSTANDING WHAT YOU READ

In this section you have read the testimony of Dr. Lamar Vest and a testimony of two experiences in New York City street ministry. Complete the following statements.

1. Lamar Vest was told that due to a growth on his vocal cords, he might never be able to _____ publicly again.
2. His approach to the problem was to go to his bedroom and _____.
3. His Bible fell open to Matthew 21:22 which says: _____.
4. On the next visit the doctor said: "There is no problem. Keep preaching and keep _____ what you have been preaching."
5. In New York City, because God's children listened to Him, obeyed, prayed and praised, He prevented a _____ and protected His children.

Answers on page 137.

Can God Answer?

The God who stopped the sun on high
                (Joshua 10:12, 13)
and sent the manna from the sky,
                (Exodus 16:4, 5)
Laid flat the walls of Jericho
                (Joshua 6:20)
and put to flight Old Israel's foe,
                (Joshua 10:8-10)
Why can't He answer prayer today
                (Luke 1:37)
and drive each stormy cloud away
                (Matthew 14:31, 32)
Who turned the water into wine
                (John 2:3-11)
And healed the helpless cripple's spine,
                (Luke 13:11-16)
Commanded the tempest, "Peace be still"
                (Mark 4:39)
And hungry multitudes doth fill?
                (John 6:9-13)
His power is just the same today—
                (Hebrews 13:8)
So why not labor, watch and pray?
                (Matthew 26:41)
He conquered in the lions' den.
                (Daniel 6:16-23)
He brought Lazarus back to life again.
                (John 11:38-45)
He heard Elijah's cry for rain
                (1 Kings 18:42-45)
And freed the sufferers from pain.
                (Matthew 8:16, 18)
If He could do those wonders then,
                (Exodus 14:21-31)
Let's prove our mighty God again.
                (Malachi 3:10)

Why can't the God who raised the dead,
                (1 Kings 17:17-22)
Gave little David Goliath's head,
                (1 Samuel 17:32-51)
Cast out demons with a word,
                (Matthew 8:28-32)
Yet sees the fall of one wee bird,
                (Matthew 10:29)
Do signs and miracles today
                (John 14:12)
In that same good, old-fashioned way?
                (Acts 5:12-16)
HE CAN! He's just the same today,
                (Ephesians 3:20)
If we believe God when we pray.
                (Mark 11:23, 24)
He's no respecter now of men—
                (James 2:1-9)
HE'LL DO THE SAME AS HE DID THEN!

This selection by an unknown author is included by Lowell Lundstrom in his book *How You Can Pray With Power and Get Results*.

Conclusion

Prayer is so profound that we can never learn all there is about it, although we study it and practice it a lifetime.

But prayer is also so simple that even a child can pray. The quick cry of "O God!" or "Lord, help!" will get a response from our heavenly Father. "Lord, save me; I perish!" prayed by the sinking Peter, brought the rescuing hand of Jesus. "Remember me, Lord, when you come into your kingdom," prayed by the thief on the other cross, brought the response, "Today you shall be with me in paradise."

A Prayer Before I Sleep

Most of us were taught as children to pray a simple prayer before we went to sleep. It went like this: "Now I lay me down to sleep. I pray the Lord my soul to keep. If I should die before I wake, I pray the Lord my soul to take. In Jesus' name. Amen."

A Prayer Before I Eat

Most of us also were taught as children to pray a simple prayer before we ate our food. We were taught to bow our head, and sometimes to hold each other's hands, and pray something like this: "Thank You for the world so sweet. Thank You for the food we eat. Thank You for the birds that sing. Thank You, God, for everything. In Jesus' name. Amen."

Or perhaps we prayed: "God is great. God is good. Let us thank Him for our food. By His hands all are fed. Thank You God for daily bread. In Jesus' name. Amen."

A Prayer Before I Die

There is a third prayer that is even more urgent for us to pray.

There is possibly nothing we do before we die more important than praying this simple prayer. It is the prayer of confession and acceptance of the forgiveness offered by Jesus. We should pray it for ourselves and then pray it with our family and friends. We often refer to it as *the sinner's prayer*. It would be good to introduce it to all persons everywhere. Such a simple prayer can change the eternal destiny of the soul.

You will find many variations of the sinner's prayer, but basically it goes like this:

"Father, I am sorry that I have sinned and offended You. I believe that Jesus is Your Son who came to earth to save us. He died in my place. I accept Him as my Savior. Forgive me. Save me. I want to live for Him now. And when this life is over I want to live in heaven with You forever. Thank You. In Jesus' name. Amen."

UNDERSTANDING WHAT YOU READ

In this passage we have looked at a quick scriptural review of some of the many acts of God in answer to prayer. We have also come to the conclusion of this study on prayer. Please complete these statements:

1. God sent _____ as food to feed the people when they prayed for food.
2. At the wedding feast Jesus turned _____ into wine.
3. In answer to Jesus' prayer and command, Lazarus _____.
4. God answered Elijah's request for _____.
5. Jesus is the _____ yesterday, today, and forever.
6. The three prayers in the conclusion are The Prayer Before I _____, The Prayer Before I _____, and The Prayer Before I _____.

Answers on page 137.

FOR FURTHER STUDY

Lundstrom, Lowell. *How You Can Pray With Power and Get Results.* Sisseton, S. Dakota: Lowell Lundstrom Ministries, 1981.

Savage, Robert. *Pocket Prayers, 777 Bible Ways to Pray.* Wheaton: Tyndale, 1982.

CONCLUSION 131

SELF-CHECK TEST

Answer the following questions without looking at the text of chapter 10. When you finish, grade yourself from the answer key on page 139.

1. Which of these are the results of prayer:
   a. God's grace in our life
   b. God's presence with us
   c. The new birth
   d. all of the above
2. Which of these are the results of prayer:
   a. transformation to the image of Christ
   b. less of self-will
   c. greater concern for the things that concern God
   d. all of the above
3. Which of these resulted from prayer:
   a. the world "turned upside down"
   b. converts in the palace of Caesar
   c. evil Corinthians made pure
   d. all of the above

These are not set forth to appear boring but to make a point and to emphasize that the lists could go on and on as to the power results of prayer.

4. Great pray-ers in the Bible were . . .
   a. Moses, David, Solomon, Elijah
   b. Genesis, Exodus, Leviticus, Numbers
   c. angels, principalities, spirits, powers
   d. all of the above
5. The missionary who experienced a great breakthrough in fighting the powers of darkness on the China-Burma border was . . .
   a. Martin
   b. Carey
   c. Fraser
   d. Livingstone
6. *Azusa Street* is the book that tells the story of the Pentecostal outpouring that came to the city of . . .
   a. Los Angeles
   b. San Francisco
   c. Chicago
   d. London

7. The poet Tennyson said that men are not much better than sheep or goats if they do not . . .
   a. read good books
   b. lift their hands in prayer
   c. learn foreign languages
   d. all of the above
8. The Villancas of Peru traveled two weeks across mountain trails to tell people in a remote village that . . .
   a. an earthquake was coming
   b. they had medicine for their sickness
   c. Jesus is the name of the Savior
   d. none of the above
9. When Lamar Vest found that he had a growth on his vocal cords, he was made well by . . .
   a. surgery
   b. chemotherapy
   c. the Word of God and prayer
   d. ignoring it
10. With the help of the Lord, I wish to make a commitment to . . .
    a. pray daily
    b. pray about everything
    c. pray the promises of God
    d. all of the above

ANSWER KEYS

For

Understanding What You Read

and

Self-Check Tests

ANSWER KEY

Understanding What You Read

CHAPTER ONE

Section 1, page 12
1. prayer
2. praying always
3. Psalms

Section 2, page 13
1. always
2. Father; Jesus
3. Paul

Section 3, page 16
1. God
2. intercessor or prayer
3. Christian
4. Corrie ten Boom

CHAPTER TWO

Section 1, page 21
1. talk
2. separated
3. hid
4. restore
5. prayer

Section 2, page 23
1. find; opened
2. will answer you
3. multitudes
4. healed

Section 3, page 27
1. Lord's Prayer
2. Presence
3. God
4. worship
5. school

Section 4, page 28
1. God
2. God's will
3. God
4. communication; prayer
5. self
6. alive; answers

CHAPTER THREE

Section 1, page 33
1. heaven; earth; God's
2. Solomon; word; promises
3. promises
4. promise
5. Joel
6. Promised
7. faithful

Section 2, page 35
1. soul happy in the Lord
2. Bible
3. meditated
4. pray

Section 3, page 38
1. joy
2. delivered
3. petitions
4. heathen
5. the Holy Spirit
6. according to His will

CHAPTER FOUR

Section 1, page 46
1. John 17
2. Not my will, but thine, be done
3. forgive
4. Psalms

Section 2, page 49
1. healed him
2. protected her
3. prepared and strengthened her

Section 3, page 51
1. directed them
2. appointment
3. Dieter; Peter

CHAPTER FIVE

Section 1, page 54
1. Our Father
2. will; thine
3. evil

135

ANSWER KEY

Understanding What You Read

Section 2, page 55
1. praise
2. singing and listening
3. Adoration, Confession, Thanksgiving, Supplication

Section 3, page 56
1. standing, kneeling, lying down, walking
2. voice
3. Jesus

Section 4, page 58
1. morning, noon, and night
2. Pray without ceasing

Section 5, page 59
1. interrupted
2. closet
3. pulling her apron over her head

CHAPTER SIX

Section 1, page 63
1. Satan, the devil
2. Jesus
3. Calvary
4. blood
5. prayer

Section 2, page 66
1. lusts or selves
2. believe
3. Sin unconfessed
4. not forgive

Section 3, page 67
1. searched
2. abundantly
3. thanksgiving; faith

CHAPTER SEVEN

Section 1, page 73
1. surprises
2. yes, no, wait; unexpected answers
3. fill it in
4. calling his daughter

Section 2, page 75
1. need of God
2. love
3. power; witnesses

Section 3, page 77
1. grace
2. work
3. loves

Section 4, page 80
1. Scripture
2. go to Bible college

Section 5, page 82
1. Joseph; Abraham
2. death; resurrection
3. the will of God
4. God's glory
5. the devil

CHAPTER EIGHT

Section 1, page 86
1. Holy Spirit
2. intercession
3. blessed, wept, cast out devils, made requests
4. example

Section 2, page 88
1. permission to go to Jerusalem and rebuild wall
2. blessings
3. prayers; songs
4. wisdom
5. interpretation of dreams and visions

ANSWER KEY

Understanding What You Read

Section 3, page 91
1. practiced
2. himself
3. *New International Version*
4. Christ; love
5. spiritual life of

Section 5, page 92
1. the Lord
2. killing each other
3. melody

CHAPTER NINE

Section 1, page 98
1. ACTS
2. Adoration; Confession
3. Bible, notebook, hymnbook, concordance
4. your choice

Section 2, pages 102
1. Thanksgiving; Supplication
2. spread forth; prayed
3. thank
4. intercession

Section 3, page 104
1. prayer list and answers, thanksgiving, insights, things to do
2. Ask, Emphasize, Interpret, Other passages, Use
3. be; do

Section 4, page 107
1. Korea
2. prayer
3. fasting
4. praise, waiting, confession, Scripture reading, watching, intercession, petition, thanksgiving, singing, meditation, listening, praise

CHAPTER TEN

Section 1, page 114
1. Christ
2. history of the whole church
3. wholeness
4. in prayer

Section 2, page 117
1. Peru
2. foot (walking)
3. weeks
4. God's name

Section 3, page 119
1. Christmas
2. preacher; church
3. valuable; unforgettable

Section 4, pages 125
1. speak (or preach)
2. pray
3. Whatsoever ye shall ask in prayer, believing, ye shall receive.
4. believing
5. riot

Section 5, page 130
1. manna
2. water
3. rose from the dead
4. rain
5. same
6. sleep; eat; die

ANSWER KEY

Self-Check Tests

CHAPTER ONE

1. c
2. d
3. b
4. c
5. c
6. a
7. b
8. b
9. a
10. d

CHAPTER TWO

1. a
2. b
3. c
4. b
5. c
6. b
7. your answer is correct
8. c
9. a
10. d

CHAPTER THREE

1. d
2. b
3. b
4. c
5. a
6. b
7. a
8. d
9. c
10. d

CHAPTER FOUR

1. T
2. T
3. F
4. T
5. T
6. T
7. F
8. T
9. T
10. T

Self-Check Tests

CHAPTER FIVE

1. F
2. T
3. T
4. T
5. F
6. T
7. T
8. F
9. T
10. T

CHAPTER SIX

1. d
2. d
3. d
4. c
5. c
6. a
7. d
8. b
9. d
10. c

CHAPTER SEVEN

1. Atonement
2. Faith
3. Right Relations
4. God's will
5. In the Spirit
6. Praise   **Right** motive
7. Position **War**fare
             Right Diagnosis
8. yes
9. no
10. wait

CHAPTER EIGHT

1. your answer is correct
2. your answer is correct
3. T
4. F (Moses)
5. T
6. T
7. T
8. F (Jerusalem)
9. T
10. F (wisdom)

CHAPTER NINE

1. d
2. d
3. d
4. b
5. d
6. d
7. b
8. c
9. a
10. d

CHAPTER TEN

1. d
2. d
3. d
4. a
5. c
6. a
7. b
8. c
9. c
10. d

Bibliography

Billheimer, Paul E. *Destined for the Throne*. Minneapolis: Bethany House, 1975.

Christenson, Evelyn. *What Happens When Women Pray*. Wheaton: Scripture Press, 1980.

Cowman, Mrs. Charles. *Springs in the Valley*. Grand Rapids: Zondervan, 1968.

Dobson, James. *Emotions: Can You Trust Them?* Ventura, CA: Gospel Light Publications, 1980.

Duewel, Wesley L. *Touch the World Through Prayer*. Grand Rapids, Michigan, Francis Asbury Press, 1986.

Dufresne, Ed. *Praying God's Word* Tulsa: Harrison House, 1986.

Eastman, Dick. *The Hour That Changes the World*. Grand Rapids: Baker, 1978.

Haden, Ben. *Pray*. Nashville: Thomas Nelson, 1974.

Huegel, F. J. *Successful Praying*. Minneapolis: Dimension Books, Bethany Fellowship, 1967.

Lawrence, Brother. *The Practice of the Presence of God*. Burlington, Ontario: Inspirational Promotions.

Lemons, David L. *Bread Upon Waters*. Cleveland, TN: Pathway Press, 1986.

Lovett, C. S. *Dealing With the Devil*. Baldwin Park, CA: Personal Christianity, 1967.

Lundstrom, Lowell. *How You Can Pray With Power and Get Results*. Sisseton, SD: Lowell Lundstrom Ministries, 1981.

McElroy, Paul S. *Quiet Thoughts*. Mount Vernon, NY: Peter Pauper Press, 1964.

M'Intyre, D. M. *The Hidden Life of Prayer*. Minneapolis: Bethany Fellowship.

Savage, Robert. *Pocket Prayers, 777 Bible Ways to Pray*. Wheaton: Tyndale, 1982.

Ten Boom, Corrie. *Marching Orders for the End Battle*. London: Christian Literature Crusade, 1969.

Torrey, R. A. *How to Pray*. Chicago: Moody Press.

Unger, Merrill F. *Biblical Demonology*. Wheaton: Scripture Press, 1952, Merrill F. Unger, 1978.

Walker, Lucille. *When You Pray*. Cleveland, TN: Pathway Press, 1983.

Wallis, Arthur. *God's Chosen Fast*. London: Victory Press, 1968.
Leadership, Spring 1985.
European Action Report
Graham, David, Christian Artists